Nuremberg – Site of the Nazi Party Rallies

Staging, Experience and Violence

NÜRNBERG
Museen der Stadt Nürnberg
Dokumentationszentrum Reichsparteitagsgelände

Exhibition catalogue
of the Documentation Center Nazi Party Rally Grounds

for Nuremberg Municipal Museums
published by Martina Christmeier and Melanie Wager

Monograph series, Nuremberg Municipal Museums, Volume 23
published by Thomas Eser

This catalogue was funded by: Stiftung zur Unterstützung
des Dokumentationszentrums Reichsparteitagsgelände

Preface

The former Nazi Party rally grounds in Nuremberg is the largest preserved ensemble of Nazi state and party architecture in the Federal Republic of Germany, its buildings a visualisation of the *Third Reich's* pretensions to power and superiority. From 1933 to 1938, they provided the backdrop for the large-scale events that constituted the annual climax of Nazi propaganda attended by hundreds of thousands of party members and avid spectators. During the 1935 rally, the so-called *Nuremberg Laws* were proclaimed, effectively institutionalising the persecution of Jews and other minorities in the German Reich, and turning the name of the city into a symbol that indelibly linked it to Nazi perpetrators, followers and fellow travellers.

The founding of the Documentation Center Nazi Party Rally Grounds in 2001 marked Nuremberg's commitment to an on-going engagement with the site's fraught history. The exhibition *Nuremberg – Site of the Nazi Party Rallies. Staging, Experience and Violence* provides the narrative framework for this engagement, charting the site's chequered history from the end of the First World War to the present day and placing the historical account within the context of the social struggles for Germany's political order in the twentieth century, the crimes of the Nazi regime, and the hesitant dealings with the Nazi heritage in the Federal Republic of Germany.

The rallies were organised and choreographed to project the Nazi regime's self-image: Führer cult, military pomp, and the oft-evoked utopia of a homogeneous, yet exclusive racial *national community* played on the yearnings of many Germans for national stature while exposing the radical nature of the regime. The exhibition explores the reasons for the popularity of the Nazi dictatorship and examines social practice taking Nuremberg's urban community as an example. In contrast, it also focuses on the fate of the victims. During the Second World War, thousands of prisoners of war and forced labourers were imprisoned on the grounds; the region's Jewish population was deported from here to the death camps in the occupied Polish territories.

The exhibition also illustrates the long process of social liberalisation after 1945, through Nuremberg's difficult and contradictory engagement with the site and its unfinished monumental buildings. As the historical events recede into the past, a significant change in remembrance culture can be observed from the postwar generation's attitude of demonstratively distancing itself from the Nazi era to the dispassionate, composed and, to some extent, ironic reception of young people today.

That it provides new insights into history and encourages individual reflection is undoubtedly a merit of the exhibition. I would like to express my thanks to the curators and all those involved in the realisation of the project.

Florian Dierl,
Director, Documentation Center Nazi Party Rally Grounds

Preis: 20 Pfennig
Reichsparteitag Nürnberg
Leo Katzenberger

Having viewed the data, we must inform you that on no condition will we print such images. This was the answer we received on ordering a lenticular print for the interim exhibition at the Documentation Center. This technique, not commonly used in exhibitions, enables one picture to show two images depending on the viewing angle. The images, a propaganda postcard and a photo of concentration camp prisoners, were to visualise the two fundamental elements – inclusion and exclusion – of the Nazi vision of *national community.*

The sensitivity of the specialist printer and clear stance against right-wing extremism that motivated the refusal, are exemplary. Fostering such social mindfulness and raising critical awareness in dealing with images is an important aim of our work at the Documentation Center. In our exhibition project, the museal context and scholarly use of the images could, of course, be clearly demonstrated. Lenticular technology enhances the presentation and is aimed at provoking discussion about the use and effect of staged images – more relevant than ever in the digital age.

This process is just one example of the curatorial approach that we adopted in the conception of the exhibition *Nuremberg – Site of the Nazi Party Rallies*. We narrate the site's history without perpetuating the staged images of Nazi propaganda and the effect they were intended to elicit. In place of official Nazi photographs, amateur snapshots have been selected to reveal different takes on the mass events. Propaganda photographs in the exhibition are placed in context, and their staging and intention explained. We also chose to leave out contemporary pictures of scale models because they were used with a propagandist intention and show monumental buildings that were never finished. Photos of the construction sites are displayed instead.

In addition to adopting a critical approach to images, our main objective was to give people center stage. Biographies show a diverse society – also in the Nazi era. People of different ages and backgrounds describe how they perceived the times in which they were living, from the *Nuremberg experience* against the backdrop of the rallies to social radicalisation and various wartime experiences of violence.

Breaking with previous approaches, we spotlight local actors and events. National history and the war period unfold from a local perspective. The influence of the rallies on Nuremberg and its inhabitants, apparent not least in the self-conception *The City of the Nazi Party Rallies,* is illustrated.

Join us on this exploration and revisit established (historical) images with a critical eye.

Martina Christmeier, Nina Lutz and Melanie Wager

1918
—33

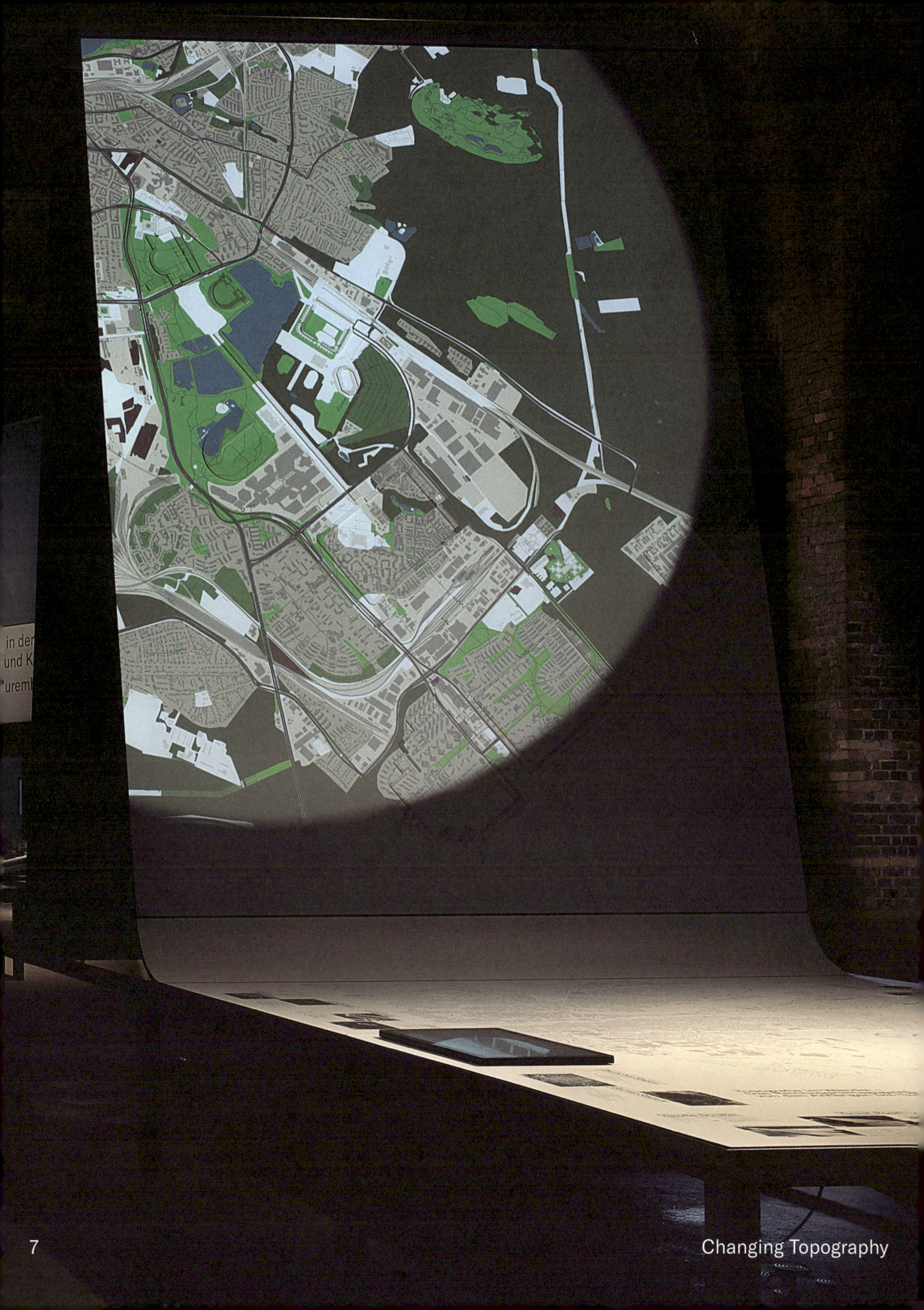

Luitpoldhain
1906 – Errichtung von Festhalle und Park zur Bayerischen Landesjubiläumsausstellung
Schauplatz von Großveranstaltungen

Kongresshalle
1935: Baubeginn der neuen, größeren Halle für den Parteikongress
1941: Kriegsbedingte Einstellung der Arbeiten, Kongresshalle bleibt ein Rohbau
Nürnberg in der
Chancen und K
Nuremb

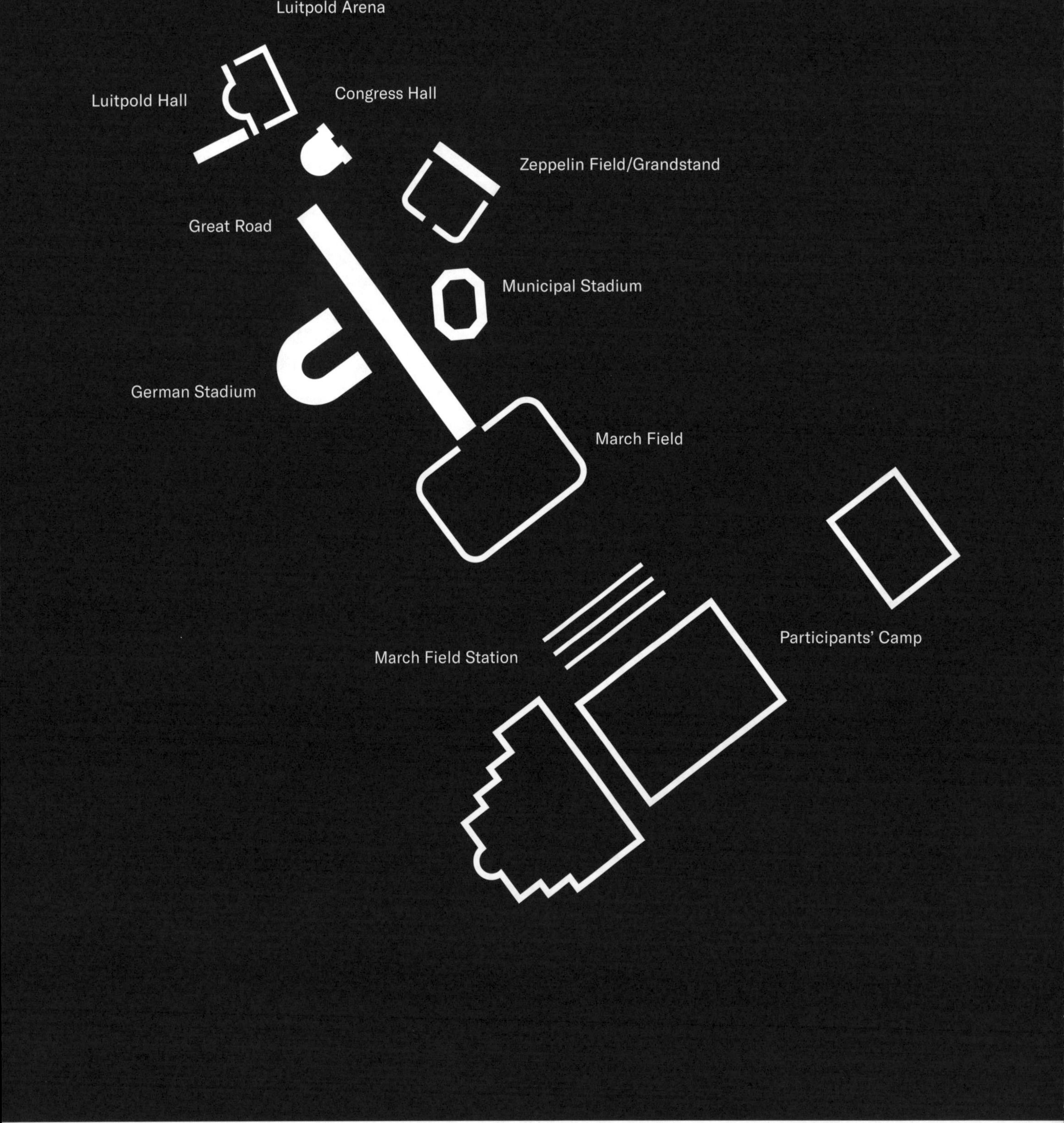
Luitpold Arena
Luitpold Hall
Congress Hall
Zeppelin Field/Grandstand
Great Road
Municipal Stadium
German Stadium
March Field
Participants' Camp
March Field Station

Luitpold Hall

Construction start	1905	Architect unknown
Building progress	1906 1937	Completion New facade for the rallies, architect Albert Speer
Use 1933–1938		Nazi Party Convention, conferences
Use after 1945	1945 1950	Destroyed (by aerial bomb) Removal, with the exception of the steps
Present-day		Car park

Luitpold Arena

Construction start	1934	Architects Walter Brugmann/Julius Schulte-Frohlinde Existing memorial from 1930, architect Fritz Mayer
Building progress	1937	Completion
Use 1933–1938		Mass roll call of the SA and SS with commemoration of the dead and consecration of the blood flag
Use after 1945	1959 1960–1963	Demolition of the grandstand, renaturation as a park, preservation of the memorial Construction of the Meistersingerhalle concert hall
Present-day		Commemorative events at the memorial, open-air concerts in the park, events in the Meistersingerhalle

Congress Hall

Construction start	1935	Architect Ludwig Ruff
Building progress	1941	Completion of the building shell without roof
Planned use		Nazi Party Convention
Use after 1945	1949/50	Use as exhibition building
	As of 1950	Rented out as warehouse to companies and clubs
	As of 1963	Rehearsal hall of the Franconian Regional Orchestra
	1969	Millions invested in conserving the building
	1972–2006	Warehouse of Quelle mail order company
	As of 2001	Documentation Center Nazi Party Rally Grounds
Present-day		Concert hall of the Nuremberg Symphony Orchestra, open-air stage in Serenadenhof, Documentation Center Nazi Party Rally Grounds, warehouse

Zeppelin Field/Grandstand

Construction start	1934	Architect Albert Speer
Building progress	1937	Completion of the main grandstand and terraces
Use 1933-1938	As of 1934	Military displays by the Wehrmacht, roll call of the Reich Labour Service, roll call of the Political Leaders (as of 1936 *Cathedral of Light*)
	1938	Sports and dance displays by various organisations
Use after 1945	1945	Demolition of the swastika by the US Army
	1950s/60s	Use as *Soldiers' Field* (for sports) by the US Army
	1967/1976	Demolition of the colonnades, removal of the side wings
	1984–2001	*Fascination and Violence* exhibition
	2000s	Decision to preserve the complex
Present-day		Various leisure, sport and music events

O Municipal Stadium

Construction start	1926	Architect Otto Ernst Schweizer
Building progress	1928 1937	Completed Wooden superstructures for the rallies
Use 1933–1938		Hitler Youth roll call
Use after 1945	Until 1961 1963–2006	US Army sports facility Multiple extensions and modernisation, collapse of the listed main grandstand
Present-day		Home ground of Nuremberg's football club, 1. FCN, use as concert venue

U German Stadium

Construction start	1937	Architect Albert Speer
Building progress	1942	Partial excavation for the foundations
Planned use		Nazi combat games
Use after 1945	1950s	Excavation pit flooded with water, rubble pit
Present-day		Silbersee and Silberbuck recreational area

Great Road

1938/39

2020

Construction start	1935	Architect Albert Speer
Building progress	1939	Partial completion of 1.5 of the planned 2 km
Planned use		Parade road for the Wehrmacht
Use after 1945	Until 1968 1990s	US Army air strip Restoration of the surface slabs, decay of the spectator stands
Present-day		Large car park

March Field

1944

2020

Construction start	1938	Architect Albert Speer
Building progress	1940	Partial completion of the grandstands and 11 of 24 towers
Planned use		Military displays by the Wehrmacht
Use after 1945	Until 1960s 1966/67 As of 1972	Use as a US Army depot Demolition of the towers Housing development
Present-day		Suburb of Langwasser

March Field Station

Construction start	1937	Architect Albert Speer
Building progress	1938	Partial completion with two tracks
Use 1933–1945	1938	Opening as station; no use during rallies
	As of 1939	Transportation of prisoners of war and forced labourers
	1941/42	Deportation of Jews from northern Bavaria
Use after 1945	Until 1988	Public transport station
Present-day		Derelict station

Participants' Camp

Construction start	1935/36	
Building progress	1939	Partial completion of camp and infrastructure
Use 1933–1945	1933–1939	Camp for SA, SS, Hitler Youth and Reich Labour Service rally participants
	1939–1945	Prisoner of war and forced labour camp, deportation assembly camp for Jews
Use after 1945	1945–1960	American internment camp, camp for displaced persons and refugees
	As of 1950s	Housing development
Present-day	Suburb of Langwasser	

"German Day"

In 1923, to the cheers of numerous honorary guests from political, aristocratic and military circles, various patriotic and völkisch organisations paraded on Nuremberg's main market square. The leading protagonists of the fledgling Nazi Party, Adolf Hitler and Julius Streicher, were prominent among them.

← *German Day* 1923
Bayerische Staatsbibliothek München/Bildarchiv
Fotoarchiv Hoffmann F.12

1918—33

1918—33 Nuremberg in the Weimar Republic – Opportunities and Crises

Nuremberg in September 1923: more than 100,000 followers of right-wing organisations gathered on the main market square. Accompanied by large-scale riots, *German Day [Deutscher Tag]* marked a nationwide breakthrough for the Nazi movement. Since its proclamation in 1918, Germany's first democracy had to repeatedly contend with assaults on its authority. The party landscape was fragmented. Broad consensus was only found in rejection of the Treaty of Versailles and there was widespread refusal to accept the country's defeat in the First World War.

It was no coincidence that *German Day* was staged in Nuremberg: the völkisch anti-Semitic faction was bent on flaunting its strength in the industrial working-class city characterised by social-democratic leanings. In the 1920s, local figures turned Nuremberg into a hub of the Nazi movement and anti-Semitism. The Republic was defended by committed local politicians. Civic society was not only politically divided – the cultural diversity of Weimar Modernism attracted both devotees and detractors. Economic recovery from 1924 onwards brought stability to the young democracy.

Nuremberg was an important venue: in 1920 the Social Democrats held a large party conference at Luitpold Grove. In 1927 and 1929 the Nazi Party held its early party conferences there.

"Socialist Workers' Youth Day"

As the traditional working-class city, Nuremberg was intentionally chosen by the Socialist Workers' Youth for their Reich Youth Day. In 1923, more than 50,000 young men and women formed a singing procession through the old town, demonstrating their support for the Republic.

← *Socialist Workers' Youth Day* 1923
Archiv der Arbeiterjugendbewegung

Urban Society in Turmoil

Struggle for the Republic

Germany's first democracy was beset by problems from the outset: massive experience of violence in the First World War and the anti-democratic attitudes of significant elements of society resulted in radical protests against the Weimar Republic – from both left and right. In Nuremberg, the political struggle erupted on to the streets and in factories during *German Day,* leaving one dead and many injured.

Alarmed, the labour movement feared that the Republic would be overthrown by völkisch organisations. They were not far wrong; the Hitler Putsch took place in Munich in November, and failed. The main instigators were arrested and the Nazi Party banned. At the beginning of 1924, the democratic parties formed the nationwide defence league *Reich Banner Black-Red-Gold [Reichsbanner Schwarz-Rot-Gold]* to protect the Republic.

Enemies of the Republic

Founded in 1918, the German national defence league *Steel Helmet, League of Front-line Soldiers [Stahlhelm, Bund der Frontsoldaten]* rejected the Treaty of Versailles and fought against the Weimar Republic, also in Nuremberg. Its symbols, the steel helmet and battle flag, were a clear reference to the German Empire and to the First World War.

↑ Badge around 1930
Garnisonmuseum Nürnberg/exhibit photography: Rudi Ott

Police Report

In 1923 the political struggle was omnipresent in Nuremberg. The police report on *German Day* listed violent riots of left and right-wing organisations. Minor incidents sparked full-scale clashes.

→ Police Report 1923
Stadtarchiv Nürnberg C 7/I Nr. 2982

öffentlichen Personenkraftwagen II N 555 am Bahnhofplatz gegen das Sterntor zu. Nächst des Prinzregentendenkmals begegneten ihnen ein Zug Nationalsozialisten, worauf Früh und Ernst aus dem Auto riefen: " Jhr Arschlöcher ". Hierauf sprangen etwa 4 - 6 Nationalsozialisten, darunter der led.Kaufmann Hans S t e i n - kirch n e r , wohnhaft in Markt-Bibart, auf das Auto und schlugen einige Fenster ein. Hierauf schlugen sie mit Totschlägern und Stöcken auf Früh und Ernst ein. Lebensgefährliche Verletzungen haben die beiden nicht erlitten. Der Haupttäter Steinkirchner wurde zur Polizeiwache IX verbracht, wobei bei der körperlichen Durchsuchung ein Revolver vorgefunden wurde. Dieser Revolver wurde beschlagnahmt und wird mit Anzeige eingeliefert. Dem Besitzer des Personenkraftwagens entstand ein Schaden von etwa 20 Millionen Mark.

Nachmittags gegen 9 Uhr ging der led.25 Jahre alte Arbeiter Hans W a l z , Gugelstraße Nr.112/II, Angehöriger der Hakenkreuzler, durch die Tafelfeldstraße stadtauswärts. Ungefähr 12 Personen, wahrscheinlich Kommunisten, die auf der entgegengesetzten Straßenseite stadteinwärts gingen, sprangen plötzlich auf Walz zu, warfen ihn auf den geklinkerten Gehsteig und gingen dann eilig davon. Walz dürfte durch den Fall nach Angabe des Herrn Dr.Obermeier vermutlich eine Gehirnerschütterung oder einen leichten Schädelbruch erlitten haben und wurde von der Mannschaft der Sanitätswache in das städt.Krankenhaus verbracht. Ob Lebensgefahr besteht , ist noch nicht festgestellt bezw. noch nicht bekannt. Die Täter sind unbekannt.

Nachmittags gegen 9.30 Uhr wurde im Cafe Königshof in der Königstraße Nr.65, von dortigen Gästen das Deutschlandlied gesungen. Es erhoben sich deshalb sämtliche Gäste mit Ausnahme des ledigen 18 Jahre alten Gütlers Leonhard S c h a t z , wohnh. in Fürth i./B., Blumenstraße Nr.4, von ihren Plätzen. Schatz wurde aufgefordert, sich zu erheben und da er dies nicht tat, wurde er von mehreren unbekannten Tätern mit der flachen Hand ins Gesicht geschlagen. Auch wurden ihm die Nähte von seinem Anzug, als er von unbekannten Personen aus dem Lokal hinausgeschoben wurde, etwas aufgerissen. Schatz erklärte, daß er keinen Strafantrag stelle und daß er die Täter nicht mehr erkennen werde.

Nachmittags gegen 10.30 Uhr stand eine größere Anzahl - etwa 80 Mann - vor der Wirtschaft zur grünen Eiche, mittl. Bleiweisstraße Nr.12, welche beabsichtigten, gegen die Wirtschaft, in welcher sich Nationalsozialisten als Gäste befanden, gewaltsam vorzugehen. Beim Eintreffen der gerufenen Polizeimannschaft zerstreuten sich zum Teil die angesammelten Personen.

Schwarz Rot Gold
Abteilung
Nürnberg

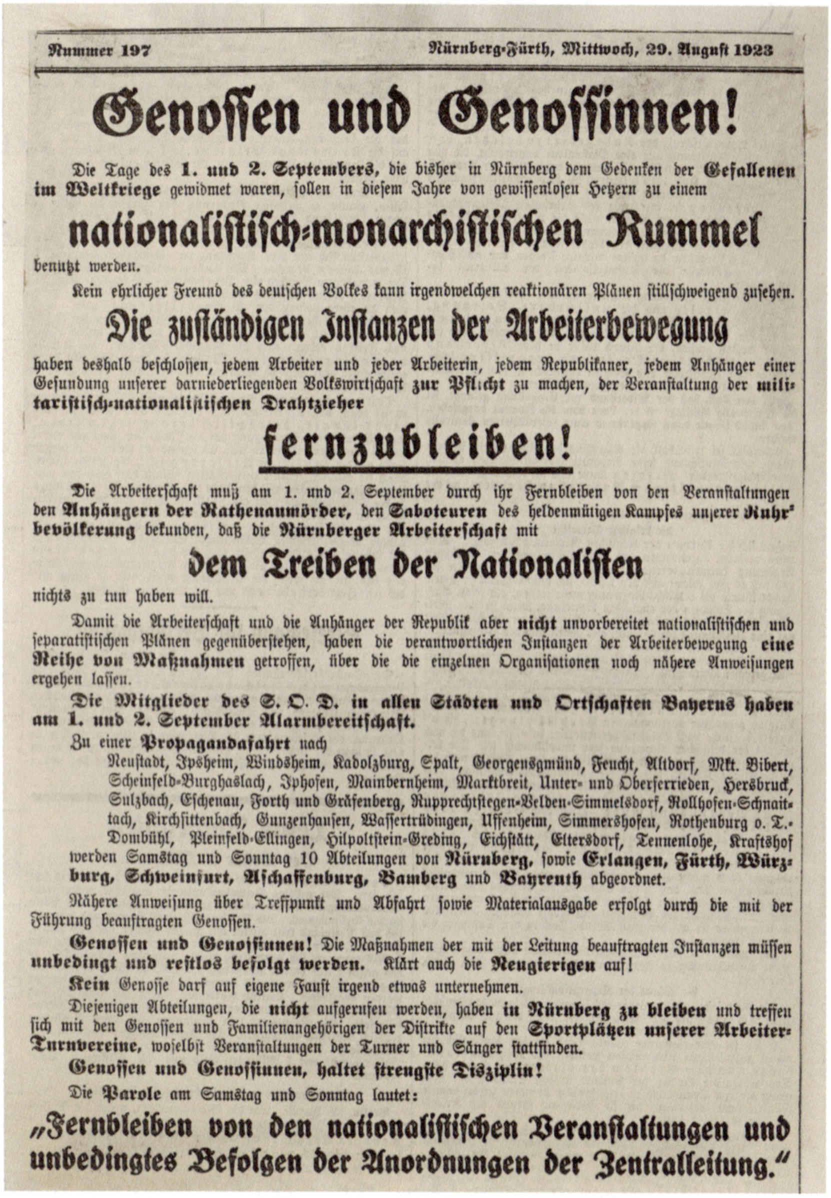

Nummer 197 — Nürnberg-Fürth, Mittwoch, 29. August 1923

Genossen und Genossinnen!

Die Tage des **1. und 2. Septembers**, die bisher in Nürnberg dem Gedenken der **Gefallenen im Weltkriege** gewidmet waren, sollen in diesem Jahre von gewissenlosen Hetzern zu einem

nationalistisch-monarchistischen Rummel

benutzt werden.

Kein ehrlicher Freund des deutschen Volkes kann irgendwelchen reaktionären Plänen stillschweigend zusehen.

Die zuständigen Instanzen der Arbeiterbewegung

haben deshalb beschlossen, jedem Arbeiter und jeder Arbeiterin, jedem Republikaner, jedem Anhänger einer Gesundung unserer darniederliegenden Volkswirtschaft **zur Pflicht** zu machen, der Veranstaltung der **militaristisch-nationalistischen Drahtzieher**

fernzubleiben!

Die Arbeiterschaft muß am 1. und 2. September durch ihr Fernbleiben von den Veranstaltungen den **Anhängern der Rathenaumörder**, den **Saboteuren** des heldenmütigen Kampfes unserer **Ruhrbevölkerung** bekunden, daß die **Nürnberger Arbeiterschaft** mit

dem Treiben der Nationalisten

nichts zu tun haben will.

Damit die Arbeiterschaft und die Anhänger der Republik aber **nicht** unvorbereitet nationalistischen und separatistischen Plänen gegenüberstehen, haben die verantwortlichen Instanzen der Arbeiterbewegung **eine Reihe von Maßnahmen** getroffen, über die die einzelnen Organisationen noch nähere Anweisungen ergehen lassen.

Die Mitglieder des S. P. D. in allen Städten und Ortschaften Bayerns haben am 1. und 2. September Alarmbereitschaft.

Zu einer **Propagandafahrt** nach

Neustadt, Ipsheim, Windsheim, Kadolzburg, Spalt, Georgensgmünd, Feucht, Altdorf, Mkt. Bibert, Scheinfeld-Burghaslach, Iphofen, Mainbernheim, Marktbreit, Unter- und Oberferrieden, Hersbruck, Sulzbach, Eschenau, Forth und Gräfenberg, Rupprechtstegen-Velden-Simmelsdorf, Rollhofen-Schnaittach, Kirchsittenbach, Gunzenhausen, Wassertrüdingen, Uffenheim, Simmershofen, Rothenburg o. T.-Dombühl, Pleinfeld-Ellingen, Hilpoltstein-Greding, Eichstätt, Eltersdorf, Tennenlohe, Kraftshof

werden Samstag und Sonntag 10 Abteilungen von **Nürnberg**, sowie **Erlangen, Fürth, Würzburg, Schweinfurt, Aschaffenburg, Bamberg** und **Bayreuth** abgeordnet.

Nähere Anweisung über Treffpunkt und Abfahrt sowie Materialausgabe erfolgt durch die mit der Führung beauftragten Genossen.

Genossen und Genossinnen! Die Maßnahmen der mit der Leitung beauftragten Instanzen müssen **unbedingt und restlos befolgt werden.** Klärt auch die **Neugierigen** auf!

Kein Genosse darf auf eigene Faust irgend etwas unternehmen.

Diejenigen Abteilungen, die **nicht** aufgerufen werden, haben **in Nürnberg zu bleiben** und treffen sich mit den Genossen und Familienangehörigen der Distrikte auf den **Sportplätzen unserer Arbeiter-Turnvereine,** woselbst Veranstaltungen der Turner und Sänger stattfinden.

Genossen und Genossinnen, haltet strengste Disziplin!

Die **Parole** am Samstag und Sonntag lautet:

„Fernbleiben von den nationalistischen Veranstaltungen und unbedingtes Befolgen der Anordnungen der Zentralleitung."

Appeal by the SPD

Threat of civil war: in August 1923 the SPD [Social Democratic Party of Germany] called upon its members to defend the Republic by legal means and to steer clear of the völkisch nationalist events during *German Day*. Not all heeded the request.

↑ Fränkische Tagespost 29.8.1923
Stadtarchiv Nürnberg C 7/I Nr. 2982

Upholding the Republic

Founded in June 1928, the Nuremberg Eibach-Röthenbach division of the democratic defence league *Reich Banner Black-Red-Gold [Reichsbanner Schwarz-Rot-Gold]* publicly demonstrated its democratic stance with a hand-sewn flag.

← Flag 1928
Property of the Lämmermann family/exhibit photography: Tim Hufnagl

Between Dix and Dürer

Modernism reached Nuremberg in the mid-1920s: a liberal zeitgeist evolved as a counterweight to the conservative mindset of the German Empire. Civic society engaged in disputes about architecture and art, tradition and avantgarde. Despite the reservations of middle-class circles, popular culture in the shape of film and vaudeville theatre also developed in Nuremberg.

Opened in 1921, the Volkshochschule adult education institute promised democratic education for all. Mayor Hermann Luppe introduced new ideas to marketing the city by illuminating historical sights. For the Dürer Year [Dürerjahr] of 1928, a cultural highlight – Luppe intentionally purchased modern art for the city. In 1930, Nuremberg's first high-rise building was opened. Made of reinforced concrete, the six-storey publishing house of the social democratic newspaper *Fränkische Tagespost* was a local example of Neues Bauen, a new architectural movement.

Neues Bauen

An example of this new architecture movement, the striking publishing house of the *Fränkische Tagespost* was dedicated in 1930. Unlike the previously opened department store of the Jewish entrepreneur Salman Schocken, the plain sober façade and innovative illumination no longer caused a stir.

↑ *Fränkische Tagespost* publishing house before 1933
Archiv Fränkische Verlagsanstalt

Public Acquisition

With its acquisition of Otto Dix's iconic picture of the New Objectivity movement, the city made a statement in the Dürer Year. Painted by Otto Dix in 1925, the *Portrait of the dancer Anita Berber* stands for the dissolute lifestyle of Berlin in the 1920s.

→ Otto Dix: *Bildnis der Tänzerin Anita Berber* 1925
VG Bild-Kunst

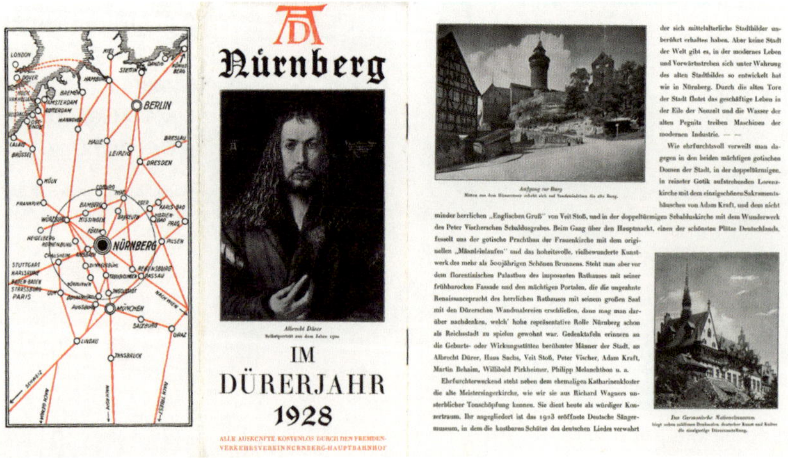

Traditional Advertising

Modernism had no place in the promotional activities for the Dürer Year in 1928, which continued to focus on traditional Nuremberg scenes of the historic city.

↑ Promotional brochure 1928
Dokumentationszentrum Reichsparteitagsgelände DZA-0109

Economy as Crisis Factor

The Republic was in the throes of an acute economic crisis in 1923. High government debts incurred by coping with the consequences of the war, and domestic unrest, led to rapid currency devaluation. Large parts of the German population were impoverished. A currency reform in November 1923 ended the hyperinflation. Germany was solvent again. Although the economy recovered slowly, it did not achieve its pre-war levels. People increasingly sought distraction in consumption and entertainment.

The Wall Street Crash in October 1929 brought the economic upturn to an abrupt end. The Great Depression resulted in massive wage cuts and a sharp rise in poverty and criminality. In Nuremberg, many companies filed for bankruptcy. Once again, radical protests from the left and right imperilled democratic order across Germany.

Economic Upturn

As of 1924, the improved economic situation enabled the population at large to enjoy a new consumption experience. Modern department stores like Kaufhaus Schocken opened in Nuremberg in the middle of the 1920s. The modern building was hotly disputed at all levels of society.

← Opening of the Schocken department store, 1926
Stadtarchiv Nürnberg A 34-1966

Nuremberg Emergency Money

In the middle of 1923, Nuremberg began to print its own emergency money to compensate for the lack of government currency. The population generally placed more trust in the emergency money issued by local authorities to counter hyperinflation than in the official currency.

← Emergency money, several bank notes 1923 (replica)
Dokumentationszentrum Reichsparteitagsgelände DZA-0110/
exhibit photography: Martina Christmeier

Great Depression 1929

Workers from Nuremberg recall the privation.

Joseph Blöth

"I had ten marks a week to pay for food and board. On some days, a lot of days, I didn't have anything to eat. [...] So really, you never had a chance to eat you fill."

Hans-Ulrich Baier

"I didn't even get unemployment benefit. [...] I made up my mind to take anything going. I got up at 4 a.m., 3.30 a.m., and went to Spittlertormauer to get a job clearing away snow for the town."

Interviews from the 1980s
Museum Industriekultur

Local Power Struggle

Guarding Democracy

Democracy in Nuremberg had many faces: men and women alike stood up to the enemies of the Republic. A bitter struggle for votes raged among the different political factions. The liberal mayor Hermann Luppe, in particular, was the victim of a relentless smear campaign by the local Nazi Party chairman Julius Streicher. The staunch Democrat defended himself in several legal actions. The success of his modern social policies and large-scale public housing programme earned Luppe national recognition.

Nevertheless, in the election year of 1924, a foothold was gained by anti-democratic forces. The Nazis took their seats on the Nuremberg city council, with Streicher and his fellow party members acting as a highly disruptive element. Only by imposing new sanctions denying them the right to speak and banning them from chambers did Luppe manage to keep the council functioning until 1933.

Demonstrating for the Republic
Last-ditch resistance to the Nazi Party: the democratic *Iron Front [Eiserne Front]*, and *Imperial Banner Black-Red-Gold [Reichsbanner Schwarz-Rot-Gold]* organisations mobilised 60,000 people to demonstrate on the Nuremberg main square in February 1933.

↑ Main square shortly before the local seizure of power, 1933
Stadtarchiv Nürnberg E 33/III Nr. 74b

Hermann Luppe on a portrait postcard 1920s

"But the future does belong to the democratic idea!"

↗ Stadtarchiv Nürnberg E 10/18 Nr. 28_1
↓ Hermann Luppe n.y., Stadtarchiv Nürnberg E 10/18 Nr. 28_1

Barber: *Can I do anything else for you, Mr Mayor?*
Mayor: *Yes, a shave, if you please. I'm fed up of the caricatures in the Stürmer, everyone recognises me by my beard.*
Barber: *Ah, now I get it. That was why Dr Süßheim was in here this morning.*

Hermann Luppe
1874–1945

The Frankfurt lawyer Dr Hermann Luppe became mayor of Nuremberg in 1920. A founding member of the liberal German Democratic party and member of the *Reich Banner Black-Red-Gold*, he resolutely supported the Weimar Republic. In the town hall, he worked constructively with the SPD faction and staunchly opposed the Nazi councillors.
In March 1933, the Nazis unlawfully imposed the Reichstag election results at local level in Nuremberg. Luppe was detained for several weeks and forced to resign. In Berlin, he worked in the resistance, being arrested frequently and kept under constant surveillance by the police and Gestapo. Luppe died in 1945, during the last air raid on his home town Kiel.

"Stürmer" Caricature

In the 1920s, Luppe and his fellow council member Max Süßheim were attacked constantly in the anti-Semitic weekly *Der Stürmer*, published by Julius Streicher. In 1926, *Stürmer* illustrator Philip Rupprecht highlighted this fact in a caricature on the cover.

← Philipp Rupprecht (Fips): Untitled caricature
in: Der Stürmer Nr. 8/1926, Stadtbibliothek Nürnberg Amb. 2. 903 (4, 1926, 1–53)

Max Süßheim in his essay
"The National Socialist Plague" 1930

"The strongest moral courage is powerless against systematically organised troublemaking and terror."

↗ Das freie Wort 9.2.1930
↓ Max Süßheim around 1928, Stadtarchiv Nürnberg C 21/VII Nr. 154_Süßheim, Max_2

Als nationale Männer regierten

Als in Deutschland nationale Männer regierten:
verbluteten in den Schützengräben Millionen;
hungerten in der Heimat Millionen;
war die Wirtschaft zerschlagen;
hatte jeder den Schrank voll „Karten";
gab es wöchentlich pro Kopf 2 Pfd. schlechte Kartoffeln;
½ Pfund Heringe;
1 Brot mit Kartoffeln;
80 Gramm Margarine;
20 Gramm Butter;
Kaffeeersatz;
200 Gramm Rübenmarmelade;
½ Pfund Mehl;
½ Pfund Nudeln (ohne Eierspur);
½ Pfund Grieß.
Denkt daran am 5. März. Denkt daran und gebt den Herren, die heute wieder regieren wollen, die einzige Antwort:
Wählt Liste 2!

Dr. Max Süßheim

Alarm!

Heute Freitag, den 3. März, abends 8 Uhr

15 öffentliche Kundgebungen

der Eisernen Front in folgenden Sälen:

Rosenau
Stadtpark
Humboldtsaal, Humboldtstraße
Leonhardspark
Patrizierkeller, Bucher Straße 137
Sängerhalle, Hummelsteiner Weg
Saalbau West, Wandererstraße
Saalbau Loher Moos
Saalbau Buchenbühl
Volksgarten Mögeldorf
Waldschänke, Frankenstraße 199
Saalbau Linde, Zerzabelshof
Saalbau Befold, Mühlhof
Gesellschaftshaus Gartenstadt
Saalbau Rangierbahnhof

Referenten:

Ammon Lina, Bardeleben Otto, Behschnitt Fritz, Brockmann Herm., Fischer Emil, Girrmann Karl, Hagen Lorenz, Hardauer Hans, Herrmann Math., Kupfer Erhard, Lowig Georg, Riepekohl Wilh., Rollwagen Hans, Schamberger Greg., Staudt Andreas

Männer! Frauen! Werktätige! Heraus zum Entscheidungskampf!

Nationalsozialisten haben keinen Zutritt. Eintritt 20 Pfg., für Erwerbslose 10 Pfg.

Kampfleitung der Eisernen Front

Gefiederte Baumeister

Der Nestbau der Vögel hat begonnen / Anpassung an die veränderten Waldverhältnisse / Die Nestarten

Max Süßheim
1875–1933

As SPD councillor and lawyer, Dr Dr Max Süßheim and many other Jewish citizens played a leading sociopolitical role in Nuremberg. In the *Luppe v. Streicher trial* in 1925, in his defence of the mayor, Süßheim was also defending democracy. In February 1930, in the face of Nazi terror and personal hostilities, he published a perceptive article entitled *Die nationalsozialistische Seuche [The National Socialist Plague]*.

Süßheim died of a heart attack at the beginning of March 1933. In his will, he expressed his deep hurt at the many personal, political and professional affronts and insults. The funeral oration for Nuremberg's most important cultural politician in the 1920s and the epitome of self-assured Judaism was held by Mayor Hermann Luppe.

Obituary
Max Süßheim's death saw the passing of a committed Nuremberg Democrat. The SPD press penned an obituary in his honour. The announcement of the Nuremberg democrats' last public gathering was printed on the same page.

← Fränkische Tagespost 3.3.1933
Stadtbibliothek Nürnberg Ztg 00125 (1933, 1–3)

Julie Meyer in her article
"The endangered status of women in the Republic" 1928

"What could be more boring than three men holding forth, one after the other, at a gathering!"

↗ Echo der jungen Demokratie Nr. 1/1928
↓ Julie Meyer n.y., property of Hiltrud Häntzschel

Public Appearances
Julie Meyer publicly voiced her democratic convictions in critiques about the role of women in politics, National Socialism and anti-Semitism.

↑ Julie Meyer speaking at an event, around 1923
Property of Hiltrud Häntzschel

Julie Meyer
1897–1970

Dr Julie Meyer was a councillor, local party chairman and co-publisher of the German Democratic Party newspaper *Echo der jungen Demokratie*. In 1933 the Nazis banned the Jewish scholar from practising her profession as a lecturer in law, labour studies and sociology. She increasingly risked her own safety through her work for the Nuremberg advice centre for persecuted Jews.

In 1937, she succeeded in emigrating to the USA, though loss of citizenship deprived her of her doctor's degree and source of livelihood. After a long struggle for survival, she was appointed professor at the *New School for Social Research* and lived in New York until her death in 1970. At her own wish, she was laid to rest in the Jewish cemetery in Nuremberg.

Center of the Nazi Movement

It was no coincidence that the Franconian Gauleiter was officially allowed to style himself as the *Franconian Leader [Frankenführer]*. Franconia was of crucial geographical and political importance to the rise of the Nazi party. At the dawn of the 1920s, Streicher in Nuremberg and Hitler in Munich were evenly-matched contenders for the leadership of the völkisch faction.

In 1922, Streicher and his party joined Hitler – to the mutual benefit of both. Streicher doubled membership of the Nazi party, paving Hitler's way in Northern Bavaria. By subordinating himself to Hitler at the right time, he secured his own position of power in Franconia, thus turning working-class Nuremberg into a stronghold of the Nazi movement as early as the mid-1920s. With its aggressive dynamic presence and benefiting from the global economic crisis, the Nazi party gained the vote of broad swathes of the electorate in the 1930 parliamentary election, although it never achieved a majority in the city council.

Old "Comrades-in-Arms"
A postcard of the 1933 Nazi Party Rally still portrayed Hitler and Streicher as a kind of dual leadership at the head of the Nazi movement, emphasising the enduring bond between the two since *German Day* 1923.

↑ Postcard *Nazi Party Rally Nuremberg 1923–1933*
Stadtarchiv Nürnberg A 5–1446

Local Seizure of Power
Adolf Hitler was appointed Reich Chancellor on 30 January 1933. On the strength of an emergency decree, the Nazis forcibly squashed political rivals and took control of the government in the states and local communities. In Nuremberg Julius Streicher headed on 9 March 1933, a procession of SA and SS men from the Deutschherrnwiese via the police headquarters, main square and city hall to the Imperial Palace. He was the first to hoist the swastika flag on a public building in a Bavarian city. The democratically elected mayor Hermann Luppe was replaced by Nazi councillor Willy Liebel.

→ March through Nuremberg 9.3.1933
Stadtarchiv Nürnberg E 39/I Nr. 1123_48_1, 49_1, 24_1, 28_1, 51_1, 35_1, 31_1, 38_1

Karl Holz to Max Süßheim
in a city council meeting 1925

“We’ll soon wipe the smile off your face.”

↗ Stadtarchiv Nürnberg C_7_IX_SRP_Nr_350_2
↓ Karl Holz n.y., Bayerisches Hauptstaatsarchiv München MInn 83866 Bildersig., Karl Holz Slg. Personen 1585

Achtung! Achtung!

„Das Warenhaus als Todfeind des schaffenden Volkes“

Über dieses Thema spricht am Montag, den 18. Oktober 1926, abends 8 Uhr

Karl Holz

in den **Humboldt-Sälen,** Humboldtstraße 116 (Steinbühl).

Karl Holz
1895–1945

A municipal employee, Karl Holz joined the Nazi party in 1922 shortly after Streicher, taking a seat on the Nuremberg city council in 1924. In subsequent years he became editor of the *Stürmer* and deputy Gauleiter. His attacks on Mayor Luppe resulted in his dismissal from public service in 1925.

In 1938, as part of the *Holz campaign*, huge numbers of expropriated Jewish-owned buildings and properties were entered under his name in the land register. This practice, deemed illegal even under Nazi law, resulted in Streicher’s removal from office and suspension from duties for Holz. His corpse was found in Nuremberg at the end of the war.

Public Speeches
Holz defamed the new department stores as the alleged *arch enemy of the working people* not only in the *Stürmer*, but also in numerous speeches, underpinned by radical anti-Semitism and the interests of localshopkeepers.

↑ Der Stürmer Nr. 42/1926
Stadtbibliothek Nürnberg Amb. 2. 903 (4, 1926, 1–53)

Julius Streicher in his script of a speech
"My proudest day. 9th of March 1933 in front of the town hall in Nuremberg"

"I have always looked forward to the day when I can report to the Führer that Nuremberg is his. Today that day has come."

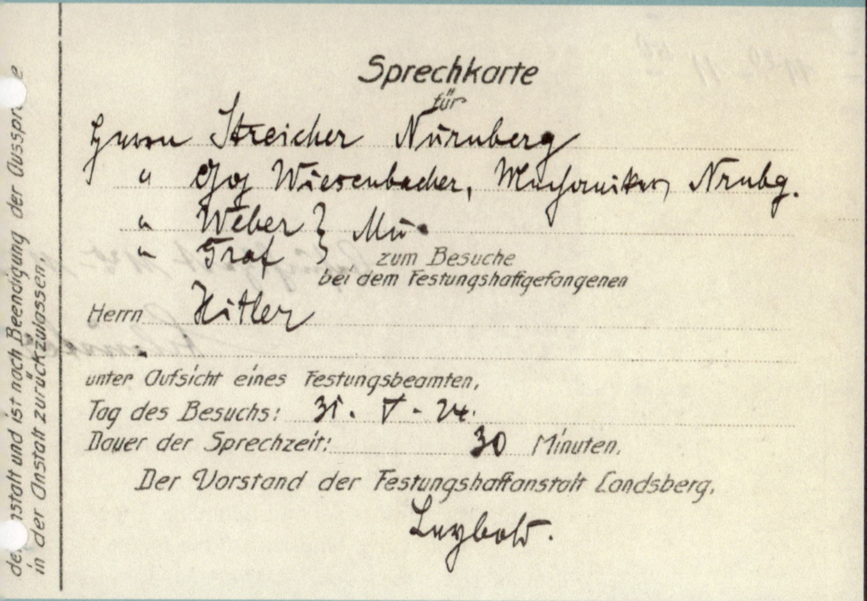

Sprechkarte
für
Herrn Streicher Nürnberg
u. Jos. Wiesenbacher, Nbg.
u. Weber } Mü.
u. Graf }
zum Besuche
bei dem Festungshaftgefangenen
Herrn Hitler
unter Aufsicht eines Festungsbeamten,
Tag des Besuchs: 31. V. 24.
Dauer der Sprechzeit: 30 Minuten.
Der Vorstand der Festungshaftanstalt Landsberg.

Permission to Visit

Following the failed attempted coup in 1923, Hitler and Streicher were given prison sentences. Released before Hitler, Streicher remained in contact with him. Together they went on to plan the future of the Nazi movement.

↑ Streicher's pass, required for visiting Hitler in Landsberg Prison 1924
Staatsarchiv München Justizvollzugsanstalten 17000/7

Julius Streicher
1885–1946

Julius Streicher founded the local chapter of the Nazi Party in Hitler's presence in October 1922. Streicher's unconditional commitment during the *Hitler Putsch* and his loyalty during the ban on the Nazi Party and its refounding paid off. In 1925 Hitler appointed Streicher as Gauleiter of Franconia. As Reich Chancellor he granted Streicher an extraordinary degree of freedom. Streicher went on to gain notoriety nationwide as an anti-Semite and publisher of the *Stürmer*.
Only when he ignored party interests and Nazi laws in his expropriation of Jewish property was he divested of power at the beginning of 1940. He was allowed to continue publishing the *Stürmer* and keep the millions it made him. In 1946 the International Military Tribunal condemned him to death.

↗ Staatsarchiv Nürnberg NS-Mischbestand Slg. Streicher Nr. 120
↓ Julius Streicher 1923, Bayerische Staatsbibliothek München/Bildarchiv, Fotoarchiv Hoffmann. Streicher, Julius

Anti-Semitic Harassment

In the wake of war debts, a new ideologically motivated racial anti-Semitism met with growing support across the country. Civic equality, upward mobility and social integration for Jewish people were still subjects of controversy in the Weimar Republic. Jews especially were blamed by many Germans for the drastic consequences of the war.

Despite isolated protests against hostilities towards its Jewish citizens, Nuremberg, where the Nazi hate sheet *Der Stürmer* was published, became an anti-Semitic bastion in the 1920s. Julius Streicher's innovative blend of radical content and entertaining gutter press in his weekly newspaper found a receptive readership, especially in Nuremberg and Franconia.

Der Stürmer
Nürnberger Wochenblatt zum Kampfe um die Wahrheit
HERAUSGEBER : JULIUS STREICHER

Nummer 43 | Nürnberg, im Okt. 1926 | 4. Jahr 1926

Dr. Hermann Luppe
und der Zwickauer Warenhausjude

Das entweihte Heldendenkmal von Goslawitz

... Ich gratuliere Ihnen recht herzlich und hoffe, daß alles nach Ihrem Wunsch hinaus gehen wird.

Die Juden sind unser Unglück!

"Der Stürmer"
Founded in 1923, Streicher used his weekly newspaper *Der Stürmer* as a public platform to launch constant attacks on Jewish people and the Republic. Compared to the attention-grabbing cover with its typical caricature, the design of the inner spreads tended to be conventional.

↑ Der Stürmer Nr. 43/1926
Stadtbibliothek Nürnberg Amb. 2. 903 (4, 1926, 1–53)

"Handbook of the Jewish Question"
Anti-Semitic publications abounded in the 1920s. Besides magazines, books especially propagated a pseudo-academic racial anti-Semitism. Theodor Fritsch published his *Handbook of the Jewish Question [Handbuch der Judenfrage]* as early as 1907. By 1945 it had run into its 49th edition.

↑ Theodor Fritsch: Handbuch der Judenfrage, Leipzig 1919
Dokumentationszentrum Reichsparteitagsgelände DZO-0173

Bernhard Kolb, chairman of the Israelite Culture Community Nuremberg, in his memoirs "The Jews in Nuremberg" 1946

"Even at that time the situation in Nuremberg and Franconia was far grimmer than in scarcely any other area in the German Reich."

Stadtarchiv Nürnberg F 5 Nr. 404b

Fränkische Tagespost 6.1.1923

"Must not this behaviour cause every decent German, whether Jew or Christian, to blush with shame?"

Stadtbibliothek Nürnberg Ztg 00125 (1923, 1–2)

Rudolf Bing, a Jew from Nuremberg, in his memoirs n.y.

"Even before the Hitler Putsch, the gravest excesses were committed in Nuremberg."

Stadtarchiv Nürnberg F 5 Nr. 494

Nürnberger Israelitisches Gemeindeblatt 1.12.1923

"Regrettably, the cowardly attacks on Jewish citizens in our city have not yet abated."

Stadtarchiv Nürnberg F 14 Nr. 50

Police Report 17.1.1920

"The anti-Semitic movement is becoming increasingly serious."

Staatsarchiv Nürnberg Polizeidirektion Nbg.-Fürth Nr. 332

Nuremberg and the Main Synagogue

In 1871, Germany accorded Jews the same legal status as its other citizens. The sense of security and self-confidence was visible in the architecture of the main synagogue, consecrated in 1874 in Nuremberg's city centre. But even before 1933, the increasingly anti-Semitic atmosphere caused more than half of Nuremberg's Jewish population to leave their home town.

↑ Main synagogue around 1900
Stadtarchiv Nürnberg A47-KS_122_26

Dutzendteich as Event Location

Tradition and Diversity

Nuremberg and the area around Dutzendteich had been a venue for mass national events since the nineteenth century. Erected in 1906, the Luitpold Hall improved the local infrastructure, as did the modern sports stadium opened in 1928. In the 1920s, Nuremberg became a symbolic stage for shows of political power. They frequently resulted in violent tussles between rival political factions.

Gatherings with more than 70,000 people were not uncommon. The participants came from all over the Republic. Singers appropriated the tradition of the City of the Master Singers for their own ends. The labour movement regarded liberally-governed Nuremberg as a republican island in conservative Bavaria. The Nazis also used the city for their propaganda purposes.

Reich Youth Day

Sporting the motto *Aspiring to New Ideas, Honouring Old Traditions*, the League of Employees' Unions [Gewerkschaftsbund der Angestellten – GDA] celebrated the tenth anniversary of the Weimar constitution with its Reich Youth Day in the old town and municipal stadium in 1929.

← Reich Youth Day programme of the GDA 1929
Dokumentationszentrum Reichsparteitagsgelände DZA-0111

“Young Socialist Workers' Day”

Climax of the *Young Socialist Workers' Day [Deutscher Arbeiterjugendtag]* in 1923 was the constitution celebration at Luitpold Grove; amid cheers from more than 50,000 youngsters, Reichstag President Löbe proclaimed: *Woe betide you Nationalists, when these masses come upon you!*

← *Young Socialist Workers' Day* at Luitpold Grove 1923
in: Verband der Sozialistischen Arbeiterjugend: Unser Weg. Bericht über das Jahr 1923. Berlin 1924, Dokumentationszentrum Reichsparteitagsgelände D-0321-05

Joint Party Convention

At the 1922 Joint Party Convention in Nuremberg, the split which had divided the Social Democratic Workers' Movement into an Independent and Majority SPD was resolved nationwide in a major celebration.

↑ Joint Party Convention of the SPD at Luitpold Grove 1922
Stadtarchiv Nürnberg E 33/III Nr. 16

Contemporary Festival Culture

As elsewhere in the 1920s, organisers of the mass events in Nuremberg employed familiar elements of contemporary festival culture. Festivals with a wide variety of political orientations resorted to typical components such as historical processions, parades in the old town, rallies festooned with flags at Luitpold Grove, mass sport performances in the stadium and torchlight processions.

Styled on *German Day*, as early as 1927 the Nazi Party established its own celebratory ritual, which was later extended to lavish proportions. It availed itself of different traditions to cultivate its image. Christian customs were instrumentalised along with military rituals, elements of popular festival culture, political expressions of the labour movement and Italian fascism.

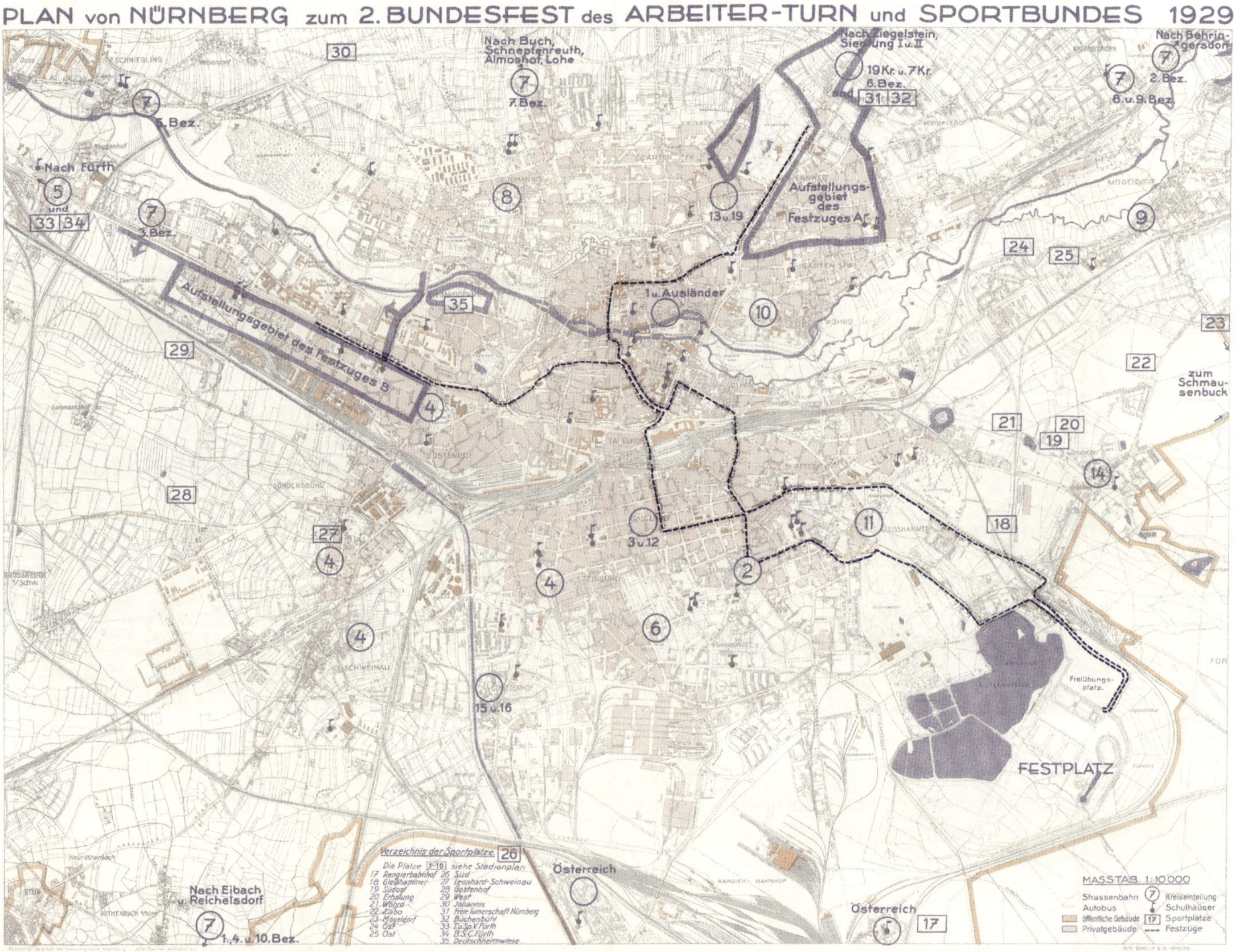

Constitution Celebration

The flag as a symbol of the respective political persuasion was an important element of all celebrations. In 1930, it also dominated the official constitution celebration staged by the city of Nuremberg at Luitpold Grove.

↑ Constitution Celebration Luitpold Grove 1930
Stadtarchiv Nürnberg A38_D_37_1

"Workers' Sports Festival"

At the *Workers' Sports Festival* in 1929, the labour movement in Nuremberg staged a public show of strength involving more than 70,000 participants; the community experience played an important role. Mass choreographies, like the one here in the stadium, were popular at the time. The Nazis drew on these when staging their rallies.

↑ Collage marking the *Workers' Sports Festival* 1929
in: Arbeiter- Turn-und Sportbund: 2. Arbeiter-Turn- und Sportfest. Gedenkblätter, Leipzig 1929, property of Alexander Schmidt

Processions

The Nuremberg population was used to processions. They always followed the same route from the old town to Dutzendteich.

← Procession plan 1929
Stadtarchiv Nürnberg C 7/I Nr. 776_17

Early Nazi Party Rallies

The favourable experiences of *German Day* prompted the Nazi Party to return to Nuremberg for its 1927 party rally, in the knowledge that it could depend on the good offices of the Nuremberg-Fürth police authority, which was sympathetic to its cause. The 1929 rally was the largest mass event hitherto staged by the Nazi Party and attracted attention beyond the boundaries of Bavaria.

The application for the 1930 rally was rejected by the city council, due to the bloody riots the year before. In 1931, the Nazi Party rejected the idea on account of the stringent requirements to be met. Apparently, a different venue was not an option. The tradition of the city as a political venue with a suitable infrastructure, the accessible location and strong regional Nazi Party support were decisive factors in Hitler's decision to hold the rallies in Nuremberg after 1933.

Luitpold Grove War Memorial

In 1930, Mayor Luppe inaugurated the municipal war memorial for the Nuremberg soldiers killed in the First World War. At their 1929 rally, the Nazis had already used the still-unfinished memorial to commemorate those who had died in the *Hitler Putsch*. However, they had to omit large sections of the planned orchestration.

↖ War Memorial in Luitpold Grove around 1930
Stadtarchiv Nürnberg A49_I-He_1767a

↗ Drawing attached to the Nazi Party rally application 1929
Stadtarchiv Nürnberg C 7/I Nr. 871_9

Complaints from the SPD

The SPD faction in the Nuremberg city council decried the violent riots that occurred during the 1929 Nazi rally, demanding consequences.

↓ Excerpt of question raised by the SPD faction
Stadtarchiv Nürnberg C 7/I Nr. 871

… organised troublemaking …

… hospitality most shamefully abused …

… life, freedom and property
of the population grievously imperilled …

… brutal acts of terror …

… many cases of assault …

… head wounds …

… provocation and abuse …

… mortal injuries …

First Rally Films

The Nazis commissioned their own rally films in 1927 and 1929, with the aim of documenting the growing strength of the movement. Although in places the events have an improvised air, the films already show Luitpold Grove in its role as central venue.

→ Film recordings of the Nuremberg Nazi Party rallies in 1927 and 1929
Institut für den Wissenschaftlichen Film G 122; G 140
(now Technische Informationsbibliothek)

1933
—39

Zeppelin Field

Zeppelin Field and a wooden grandstand opposite the present-day Zeppelin Grandstand: the 1933 rally viewed through the camera lens of an amateur photographer. Obstructed views and rubbish in the ranks of spectators were part of the experience.

↙ Zeppelin Field 1933
Dokumentationszentrum Reichsparteitagsgelände Ph-0014-04

Zeppelin Grandstand

Aside from the Luitpold Arena, the Zeppelin Grandstand and parade ground was the only venue completed. In contrast to the propaganda films, private photographs showed the rallies from the spectators' point of view. Endless hours of waiting in all weathers was also part of the experience.

↓ Zeppelin Grandstand 1938
Dokumentationszentrum Reichsparteitagsgelände D-0314-01

1933—39 The Nazi Party Rallies – Community and Exclusion

Nuremberg, September 1933: The first rally after the seizure of power once more took place in Nuremberg – Hitler having decided that the city was to be the permanent venue and *City of the Nazi Party Rallies [Stadt der Reichsparteitage]*. Henceforth a major national event, programme, length and dimension were massively upscaled. The staging focused on the rally experience. It was designed to convey the Nazi regime's key messages and promise Germany's rise again on the basis of national unity under strong leadership. The 1935 rally provided the political stage for the proclamation of the *Nuremberg Laws*, the 1938 rally for the celebration of Austria's *annexation*.

The first construction projects began in 1933. Based on plans by architect Albert Speer, as of 1934 the existing venue was to be transformed and extended into a huge cultic complex. From 1938 onwards, large-scale supplies of granite from concentration camps were planned.

Modern media techniques were to be deployed to let the nation share the community experience inspired by the rallies. The photographer Heinrich Hoffmann and film director Leni Riefenstahl shaped the image of the rallies. International reactions ranged from enthusiasm to rejection. Due to the planned attack on Poland, the 1939 *Rally of Peace* was cancelled just before the opening.

Old Town Buzz

The elaborately festooned old town and the famous sights were an established attraction for rally visitors. During the rally week, the streets and squares were thronged with people.

↙ Old Town Nuremberg 1938
Dokumentationszentrum Reichsparteitagsgelände D-0314-02

"Triumph of the Will"

Seemingly endless columns of marching soldiers dominated the propaganda film of the 1934 rally. In *Triumph of the Will* the filmmaker Leni Riefenstahl went to great lengths to create the *ideal* rally but the event never took place as she portrayed it.

↓ Leni Riefenstahl: *Triumph des Willens* 1935
Bundesarchiv Berlin

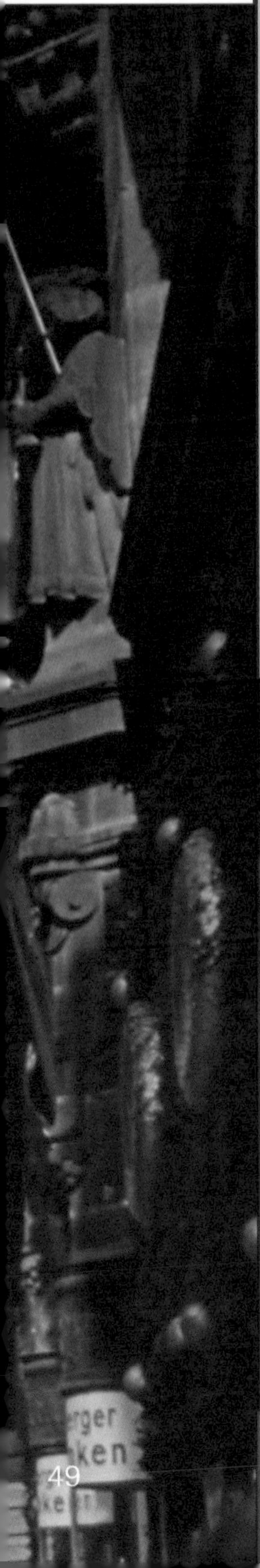

Major National Event

From Party Rally to National Celebration

The 1933 rally represented a watershed. The Nazi Party was no longer one of many; party and state had become one – and the rallies an official state occasion. As of 1934, access to financial and human resources enabled a significant professionalisation. New groups of participants extended the temporal and spatial scope of the event.

During the rally week, exceptional circumstances prevailed in Nuremberg. Up to one million participants and spectators, mainly from Germany but also from abroad, demanded an increasing amount of organisation. A special rally department and other municipal offices cooperated with the Nazi Party coordination department to prepare for and stage the mass events.

Rush for Trams and Beer

Although participants and spectators praised the organisation, typical problems associated with large-scale events gave cause for complaint. Perennial issues included overcrowded public transport, dirty accommodation, a lack of washroom facilities and also excessive alcohol consumption.

← Rinsing beer tankards 1934
Süddeutsche Zeitung Photo/Scherl Mediennr. 00338611

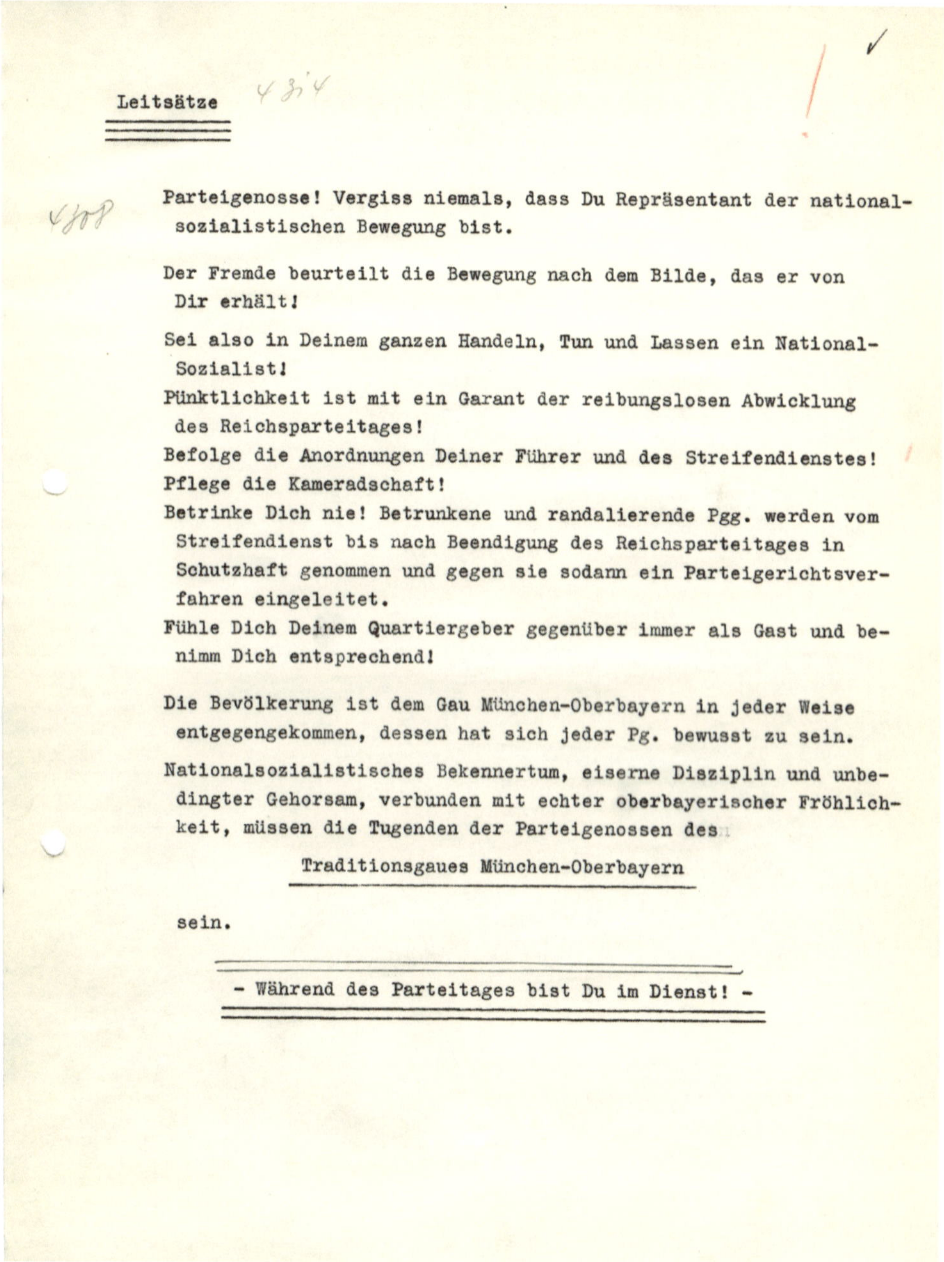

Leitsätze

Parteigenosse! Vergiss niemals, dass Du Repräsentant der nationalsozialistischen Bewegung bist.

Der Fremde beurteilt die Bewegung nach dem Bilde, das er von Dir erhält!

Sei also in Deinem ganzen Handeln, Tun und Lassen ein National-Sozialist!

Pünktlichkeit ist mit ein Garant der reibungslosen Abwicklung des Reichsparteitages!

Befolge die Anordnungen Deiner Führer und des Streifendienstes!

Pflege die Kameradschaft!

Betrinke Dich nie! Betrunkene und randalierende Pgg. werden vom Streifendienst bis nach Beendigung des Reichsparteitages in Schutzhaft genommen und gegen sie sodann ein Parteigerichtsverfahren eingeleitet.

Fühle Dich Deinem Quartiergeber gegenüber immer als Gast und benimm Dich entsprechend!

Die Bevölkerung ist dem Gau München-Oberbayern in jeder Weise entgegengekommen, dessen hat sich jeder Pg. bewusst zu sein.

Nationalsozialistisches Bekennertum, eiserne Disziplin und unbedingter Gehorsam, verbunden mit echter oberbayerischer Fröhlichkeit, müssen die Tugenden der Parteigenossen des

Traditionsgaues München-Oberbayern

sein.

\- Während des Parteitages bist Du im Dienst! -

Reichsparteitag 1935 — Organisationsleitung, Quartieramt G.

Quartierschein für Freiquartier.

Quartiergeber: 1 Zimmer mit 2 Bett(en)

Herr/Frau Paul Bayer — Beruf: Stadtrat u.Gen.Dir

Nürnberg, Nunnenbeck Straße Nr. 5 /2.Stock

mit Frühstück — Ortsgr.: Wöhrd

Quartiernehmer:

Herr/Frau Johann Engel m.Frau — Beruf: Stadtrat

in Berlin, Straße Nr.

Gau Gross-Berlin — Ortsgruppe

Der anhängende Quartierbestätigungsschein ist dem Quartiergeber sofort ausgefüllt zu übersenden

Everything according to Plan

Instruction flyers and plans abounded during the rally week, on everything from marching formations to guidelines for party members. Only holders of a billet enjoyed accommodation in one of the coveted private and mass lodgings in the region.

↑ *Conduct rules* pamphlet from the Munich-Upper Bavaria Gau 1935
Staatsarchiv München NSDAP 108

← Billet document for free accommodation with breakfast 1935
Dokumentationszentrum Reichsparteitagsgelände DZA-0068

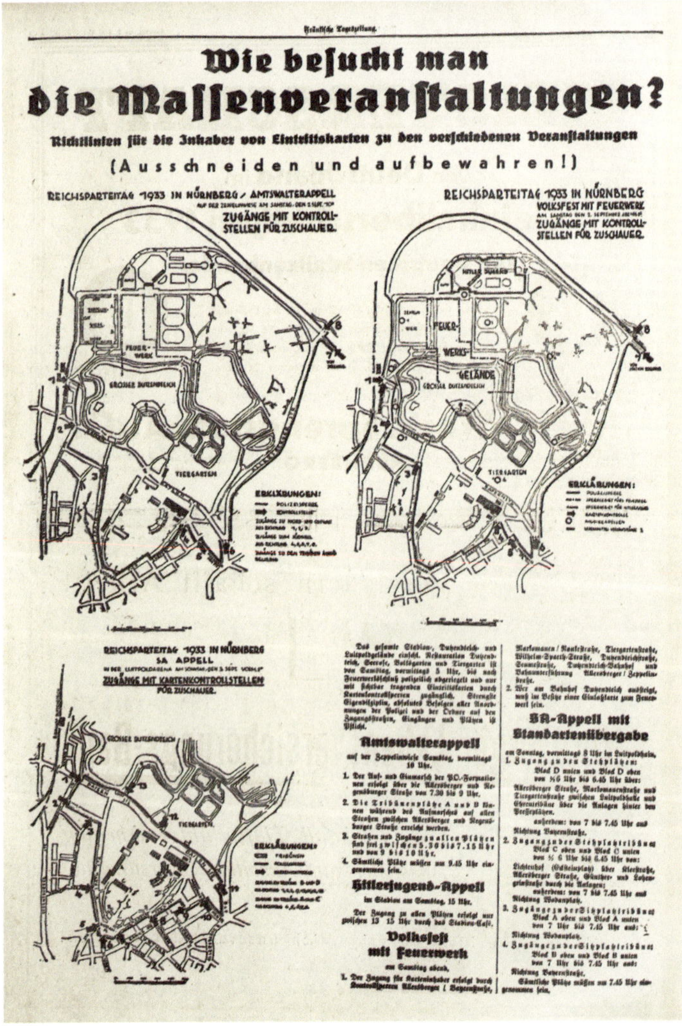

Fränkische Tageszeitung.

Wie besucht man die Massenveranstaltungen?

Richtlinien für die Inhaber von Eintrittskarten zu den verschiedenen Veranstaltungen

(Ausschneiden und aufbewahren!)

REICHSPARTEITAG 1933 IN NÜRNBERG / AMTSWALTERAPPELL
ZUGÄNGE MIT KONTROLLSTELLEN FÜR ZUSCHAUER.

REICHSPARTEITAG 1933 IN NÜRNBERG
VOLKSFEST MIT FEUERWERK
ZUGÄNGE MIT KONTROLLSTELLEN FÜR ZUSCHAUER.

REICHSPARTEITAG 1933 IN NÜRNBERG
SA APPELL
ZUGÄNGE MIT KARTENKONTROLLSTELLEN FÜR ZUSCHAUER.

Das gesamte Stadion-, Dutzendteich- und Luitpoldgelände einschl. Restauration Dutzendteich, Seerose, Volksgarten und Tiergarten ist von Samstag, vormittags 5 Uhr, bis nach Feuerwerksschluß polizeilich abgeriegelt und nur mit sichtbar tragenden Eintrittskarten durch Kartenkontrollsperren zugänglich. Strengste Eigendisziplin, absolutes Befolgen aller Anordnungen der Polizei und der Ordner auf den Zugangsstraßen, Eingängen und Plätzen ist Pflicht.

Amtswalterappell

auf der Zeppelinwiese Samstag, vormittags 10 Uhr.

1. Der Auf- und Einmarsch der PO.-Formationen erfolgt über die Allersberger und Regensburger Straße von 7.30 bis 9 Uhr.
2. Die Tribünenplätze A und B können während des Aufmarsches auf allen Straßen zwischen Allersberger und Regensburger Straße erreicht werden.
3. Straßen und Zugänge zu allen Plätzen sind frei zwischen 5.30 bis 7.15 Uhr und von 9 bis 10 Uhr.
4. Sämtliche Plätze müssen um 9.45 Uhr eingenommen sein.

Hitlerjugend-Appell

im Stadion am Samstag, 15 Uhr.

Der Zugang zu allen Plätzen erfolgt nur zwischen 13 15 Uhr durch das Stadion-Café.

Volksfest mit Feuerwerk

am Samstag abend.

1. Der Zugang für Karteninhaber erfolgt durch Kontrollsperren Allersberger / Bayernstraße, Markomanen / Rankestraße, Tiergartenstraße, Wilhelm-Spaeth-Straße, Dutzendteichstraße, Zeumestraße, Dutzendteich-Bahnhof und Bahnunterführung Allersberger / Zeppelinstraße.
2. Wer am Bahnhof Dutzendteich aussteigt, muß im Besitze einer Einlaßkarte zum Feuerwerk sein.

SA-Appell mit Standartenübergabe

am Sonntag, vormittags 8 Uhr im Luitpoldhain.

1. Zugang zu den Stehplätzen: Block D unten und Block D oben von ½6 Uhr bis 6.45 Uhr über: Allersberger Straße, Markomanenstraße und Tiergartenstraße zwischen Luitpoldhalle und Ehrentribüne über die Anlagen hinter den Presseplätzen. außerdem: von 7 bis 7.45 Uhr aus Richtung Bayernstraße.
2. Zugang zu der Stehplatztribüne Block C oben und Block C unten von ½ 6 Uhr bis 6.45 Uhr von: Lichtenhof (Gudrunplatz) über Kiefstraße, Allersberger Straße, Günther- und Lohengrinstraße durch die Anlagen; außerdem: von 7 bis 7.45 Uhr aus Richtung Wodanplatz.
3. Zugänge zu der Sitzplatztribüne Block A oben und Block A unten von 7 Uhr bis 7.45 Uhr aus: Richtung Wodanplatz.
4. Zugänge zu der Sitzplatztribüne Block B oben und Block B unten von 7 Uhr bis 7.45 Uhr aus: Richtung Bayernstraße.

Sämtliche Plätze müssen um 7.45 Uhr eingenommen sein.

“What to heed when attending the mass events”

This was the title of a full-page article in the Nuremberg Nazi daily newspaper, to *cut out and keep.* Good advice – considering the strict admission times and fixed entrances to the individual events.

↑ Fränkische Tageszeitung 2.9.1933
Stadtbibliothek Nürnberg Ztg 00113 (1933, 9–10)

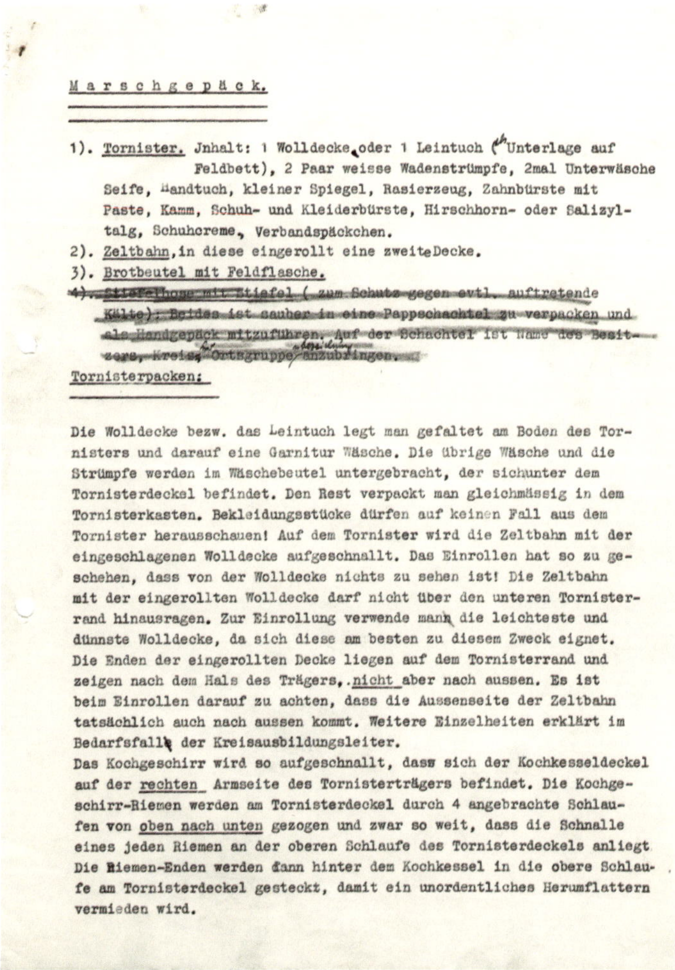

Marschgepäck.

1). Tornister. Jnhalt: 1 Wolldecke, oder 1 Leintuch (als Unterlage auf Feldbett), 2 Paar weisse Wadenstrümpfe, 2mal Unterwäsche Seife, Handtuch, kleiner Spiegel, Rasierzeug, Zahnbürste mit Paste, Kamm, Schuh- und Kleiderbürste, Hirschhorn- oder Salizyltalg, Schuhcreme, Verbandspäckchen.
2). Zeltbahn, in diese eingerollt eine zweite Decke.
3). Brotbeutel mit Feldflasche.
~~4). Stiefelhose mit Stiefel (zum Schutz gegen evtl. auftretende Kälte): Beides ist sauber in eine Pappschachtel zu verpacken und als Handgepäck mitzuführen. Auf der Schachtel ist Name des Besitzers, Kreis, Ortsgruppe anzubringen.~~

Tornisterpacken:

Die Wolldecke bezw. das Leintuch legt man gefaltet am Boden des Tornisters und darauf eine Garnitur Wäsche. Die übrige Wäsche und die Strümpfe werden im Wäschebeutel untergebracht, der sich unter dem Tornisterdeckel befindet. Den Rest verpackt man gleichmässig in dem Tornisterkasten. Bekleidungsstücke dürfen auf keinen Fall aus dem Tornister herausschauen! Auf dem Tornister wird die Zeltbahn mit der eingeschlagenen Wolldecke aufgeschnallt. Das Einrollen hat so zu geschehen, dass von der Wolldecke nichts zu sehen ist! Die Zeltbahn mit der eingerollten Wolldecke darf nicht über den unteren Tornisterrand hinausragen. Zur Einrollung verwende man die leichteste und dünnste Wolldecke, da sich diese am besten zu diesem Zweck eignet. Die Enden der eingerollten Decke liegen auf dem Tornisterrand und zeigen nach dem Hals des Trägers, nicht aber nach aussen. Es ist beim Einrollen darauf zu achten, dass die Aussenseite der Zeltbahn tatsächlich auch nach aussen kommt. Weitere Einzelheiten erklärt im Bedarfsfall der Kreisausbildungsleiter.
Das Kochgeschirr wird so aufgeschnallt, dass sich der Kochkesseldeckel auf der rechten Armseite des Tornisterträgers befindet. Die Kochgeschirr-Riemen werden am Tornisterdeckel durch 4 angebrachte Schlaufen von oben nach unten gezogen und zwar so weit, dass die Schnalle eines jeden Riemen an der oberen Schlaufe des Tornisterdeckels anliegt. Die Riemen-Enden werden dann hinter dem Kochkessel in die obere Schlaufe am Tornisterdeckel gesteckt, damit ein unordentliches Herumflattern vermieden wird.

“Perfectly” Staged

The kit bag was a symbol of the uniformed masses and the subject of detailed packing instructions. The entire rally week was planned in the minutest detail, nothing was left to chance. Party members, on duty throughout the rally, were subject to strict codes of conduct and dress which were not always easy to follow. Despite all efforts, the *perfect* rally remained a figment of elaborately staged propaganda pictures.

↑ Marching-kit instructions from the Munich-Upper Bavaria Gau 1935
Staatsarchiv München NSDAP 108

→ SA and SS in Luitpold Arena at party rally 1935
The U.S. National Archives and Records Administration Identifier 558778/ Charles Russell

Eight Days in September – Staging and Development of the Rallies

Comparing the 1933 and 1938 programmes shows how the rallies developed. Marches and parades of the Nazi organisations on the rally grounds and in the old town were an established element of the staged spectacle. While the Luitpold Arena and Zeppelin Field remained the main venues, changes were made, above all to the staging and length of the events. Their leisure and entertainment value was greatly enhanced. In 1933 the spectacle lasted five days, in 1934 seven and from 1937 onwards, eight full days.

Hanns Kerrl (Hg.): Reichstagung in Nürnberg 1938, Berlin 1939

Monday, 5 September 1938
Day of Welcome
× Hitler's arrival in Nuremberg
× Reception in the main chamber of the town hall
× Gala performance of the Master Singers of Nuremberg at the opera house

Tuesday, 6 September 1938
Opening Day of the Party Rally
× Opening of the party congress in the Luitpold Hall
× Numerous special events such as the cultural conference with the award of the German National Prize for Art and Science, took place throughout the rally week

Wednesday, 7 September 1938
Day of the Reich Labour Service
× Roll call of the Reich Labour Service on the Zeppelin Field

Thursday, 8 September 1938
Day of Community
× Sport and dance performances by various groups on the Zeppelin Field
× Nazi combat games

Friday, 9 September 1938
Day of the Political Leaders
× Roll call of the political leaders on the Zeppelin Field

Saturday, 10 September 1938
Day of the Hitler Youth
× Finals of the Nazi combat games in the Municipal Stadium
× Hitler Youth roll call in the Municipal Stadium
× Main fun fair day in the KDF village, gala concert on Adolf Hitler Square, fireworks at Dutzendteich lake

Sunday, 11 September 1938
Day of the Stormtroopers
× Massed roll call of the SA and SS in Luitpold Grove
× March-past on Adolf Hitler Square

Monday, 12 September 1938
Day of the Wehrmacht
× Wehrmacht display on the Zeppelin Field
× Conclusion of the party congress in the Luitpold Hall
× Grand Tattoo of the Wehrmacht in the presence of Adolf Hitler

Photographs of the 1938 rally

Hermann Kettler, a 36-year-old political leader from Bremen, recorded his personal impressions of the rally in a twelve double-page photo album.

↓ Private photo album Reichsparteitag 1938
Stadtarchiv Bremen 10.b-al-105

Festlich geschmücktes Nürnberg
Vor dem „Deutschen Hof"

REICHSPARTEITAG
1938
Mittwoch
7. Sept., 10 Uhr
Zeppelinwiese
Reichsarbeitsdienst
Appell und Vorbeimarsch
Zugang über Ludendorffstraße oder Dutzendteichstraße, Herzogstraße und Seumestraße. Straßenbahnen 2, 11, 12, 22, 82, 41 mit Haltestelle Dutzendteich. — Die Plätze müssen bis 9.30 Uhr eingenommen sein. — Karten werden bei verspätetem Eintreffen nicht zurückgenommen.
Block V
Tribüne Sitzplatz
A
4808
Einfahrt des Führers
Vorbeimarsch der Arbeitsgaue

N.S.K.K. rastet.

S.S. - Standarten marschieren aus

Reichsparteitag
Ausweis
FÜR AKTIVE TEILNEHMER DES
Reichsparteitages
19
38
INHABER HAT DIESE KARTE IMMER BEI SICH ZU FÜHREN

Empfang auf dem
Hugenottenplatz
Erlangen

Social Aims

The Nazi regime used the rallies as a form of political *event marketing* to pursue key social aims. Nazism was not intended to be discussed or understood, but primarily to be experienced. The rally was designed to present the national unity of the Germans regardless of class and regional differences, and to stage the consensus between the *national community* and the *Führer*.

More than just a propaganda show, the sense of community inspired by the rally was intended to reinforce identification with the Nazi state and permeate everyday life. The promises of new national strength met with wide approval and eagerness to be part of the experience. The paramilitary character of the mass event was aimed at mobilising the people mentally, in an emotional preparation for war.

“National Community” as an Exclusive Society

One people, one Reich, one Führer [Ein Volk, ein Reich, ein Führer] – this was not only a propaganda slogan to broad swathes of the crisis-ridden German population, but the yearned-for new form of society and government for a better future under strong leadership. The Nazi idea of the *national community* was based on the radical exclusion of so-called *anticommunity elements, traitors of the people* and ideologically defined minorities.

The photo reportage of July 1933 portrayed concentration camp internment as a successful way of re-educating political opponents to become members of the *national community*. Although a propaganda photo, there is no mistaking the inhuman treatment of the prisoners in Dachau. Since the majority of Germans benefited personally from the new circumstances, the violence was accepted or consciously repressed.

↙ Postcard *Party Rally Nuremberg* n.y.
Dokumentationszentrum Reichsparteitagsgelände Ph-1080-08

↘ Münchner Illustrierte Presse 16.7.1933
Deutsches Historisches Museum/S. Ahlers Inv.-Nr. Do2 95/2880

Thousands of men stand in perfect ranks on the Zeppelin Field. [...] Hella watches Hitler, who tilts his head towards the microphone almost imperceptibly. The Führer says nothing, he waits until complete silence prevails. Then he calls out in a resounding voice: “Hail my workers!” His words echo in the warm air. Thousands of young men respond fervently in unison: “Hail our Führer!” […] Hella is captivated by the hypnotic power of these words, which seem to form magical incantations and leave no room for doubt. Only certainties. The air is alive with the passion generated by thousands of people who firmly believe in fighting the fight together and are willing to shed their blood for their country.

Description of the Reich Labour Service roll call 1936
in: Lilli Gruber: Das Erbe. Die Geschichte meiner Südtiroler Familie, Mailand 2012

↑ Hitler in front of the Reich Labour Service on the Zeppelin Field 1936
in: Hanns Kerrl (Hg.): Reichstagung in Nürnberg 1936. Berlin 1937,
Dokumentationszentrum Reichsparteitagsgelände D-0329-01

Political Platform

Targeted political messages were communicated at the rallies. From 1935 onwards, the respective rally motto reflected specific domestic or foreign activities or events. The reintroduction of conscription, passing of the *Nuremberg Laws* and the *annexation* of Austria were not debated, but celebrated.

This obvious endorsement devoid of any criticism by participants and spectators served as a legitimation of the right to govern. The Nazi regime demonstrated its pretensions as a major power in the form of military shows of prowess. This display of power and strength for domestic and international audiences was one of the fundamental functions of the rallies.

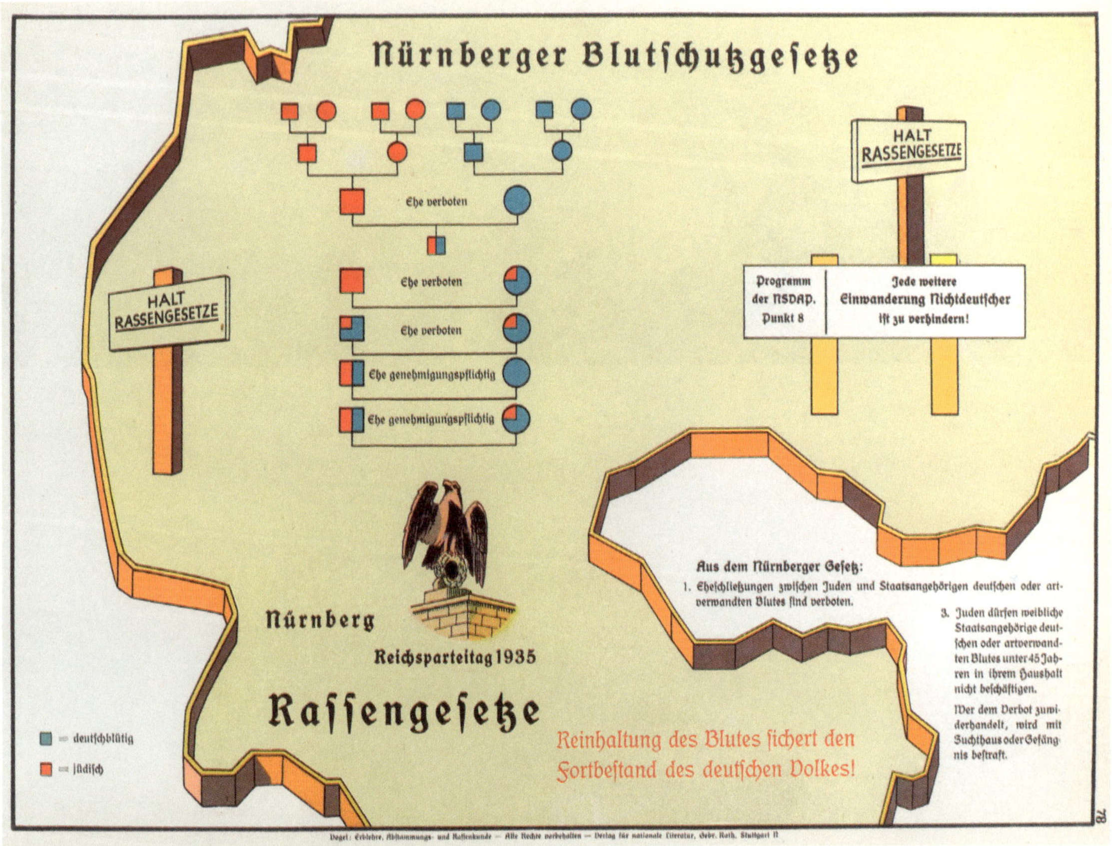

The "Nuremberg Laws"
Hermann Göring proclaimed the *Nuremberg Laws* on 15 September during the 1935 rally. The Nazi State thus illegalised relationships between Jews and non-Jews. The *Reich Citizenship Law [Reichsbürgergesetz]* degraded Jews to second-class citizens. This disenfranchisement heralded the legally endorsed persecution of Jews, Sinti and Roma and was to culminate in their mass murder.

↑ *The Nuremberg Blood Protection Laws* 1935
Bildagentur Preußischer Kulturbesitz/Staatsbibliothek zu Berlin Bild-Nr. 00040573

↓ Leo Katzenberger around 1942, Yad Vashem file number 10548/1

Leo Katzenberger
1873–1942

As Nuremberg businessman and temporarily chairman of the Jewish Cultural Organisation, Leo Katzenberger was an early victim of defamatory campaigns in the *Stürmer*. Denounced in 1942 by tenants, due to an alleged relationship with another lodger Irene Seiler, he became caught in the crosshairs of Dr. Oswald Rothaug, director of the Nuremberg special court.

The *Blood Protection Law [Blutschutzgesetz]* of 1935 did not envisage the death penalty. However, the prosecution linked *racial defilement* with special law relating to wartime, enabling Rothaug to sentence Katzenberger to death. On 3 June 1942 the sentence was carried out in Munich's Stadelheim Prison – an unequivocal case of judicial murder. Irene Seiler was sentenced to two years in prison.

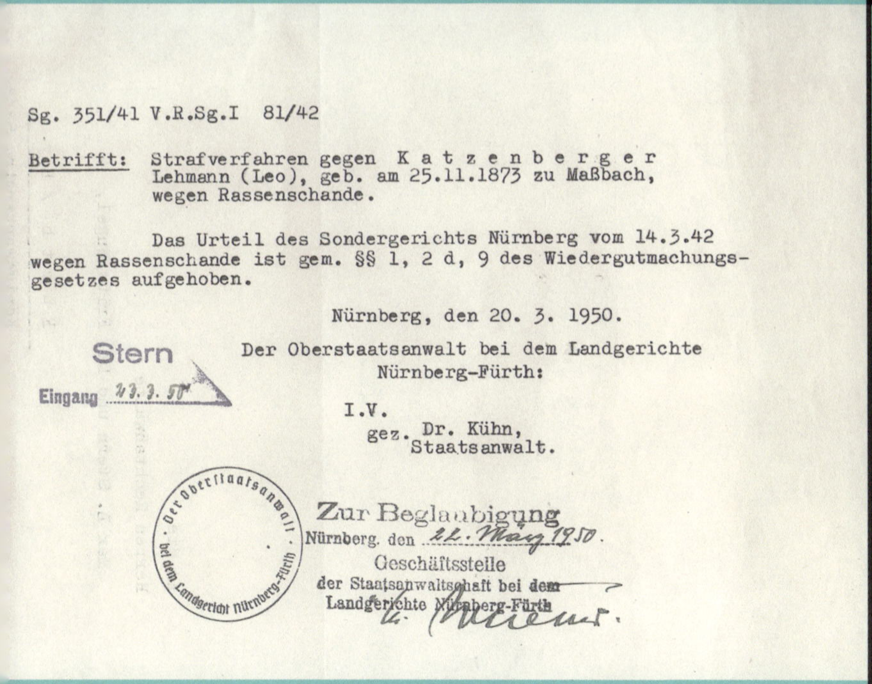

Sg. 351/41 V.R.Sg.I 81/42

Betrifft: Strafverfahren gegen K a t z e n b e r g e r Lehmann (Leo), geb. am 25.11.1873 zu Maßbach, wegen Rassenschande.

Das Urteil des Sondergerichts Nürnberg vom 14.3.42 wegen Rassenschande ist gem. §§ 1, 2 d, 9 des Wiedergutmachungsgesetzes aufgehoben.

Nürnberg, den 20. 3. 1950.

Stern

Eingang 23.3.50

Der Oberstaatsanwalt bei dem Landgerichte Nürnberg-Fürth:

I.V.
gez. Dr. Kühn,
Staatsanwalt.

Der Oberstaatsanwalt bei dem Landgericht Nürnberg-Fürth

Zur Beglaubigung
Nürnberg, den 22. März 1950.
Geschäftsstelle
der Staatsanwaltschaft bei dem Landgerichte Nürnberg-Fürth

Rehabilitation

Eight years later, Leo Katzenberger was rehabilitated by the Nürnberg-Fürth public prosecution department when it repealed the death sentence. Rothaug, sentenced to life imprisonment in the 1947 Judges Trial, was a free man by 1956. His colleagues escaped punishment entirely.

↑ Revocation notice 20.3.1950
Staatsarchiv Nürnberg AG Fürth Nachlassakt VI 1063/42

“Nuremberg Experience”

Nuremberg experience refers to the way in which people personally experienced the rallies. First-hand reports and personal memories played an important role for *Nuremberg rally-goers* and also for those who stayed at home. Testimonies in the form of letters, reports, diary entries and private photo albums reveal a wide variety of reactions to the rallies, yet fall short of allowing any clear assertions or explanations: not every enthusiastic participant believed in the misanthropic world view, not every deprecating remark spelled opposition to the Nazis.

Drawings: Hamed Eshrat

Herta, 10 years old, from Nuremberg, on the rallies in general

“In ’34 and ’35 [...], during the rallies we went to the forest [..], took food with us and looked for a nice spot somewhere because my parents said that they wanted to avoid the tumult in the city...”

Contemporary witness interview 1997
Dokumentationszentrum Reichsparteitagsgelände/Reiner Holzemer

Arno, 10 years old, from Nuremberg, on the rallies in general

“We youngsters went from one synagogue to the other, chopping and changing. [...] Pushing through the crowds, prayer book in hand, was quite an adventure, because we knew for sure that all hell would be let loose if we were caught with a Jewish prayer book under our arm.”

Contemporary witness interview 1997
Dokumentationszentrum Reichsparteitagsgelände/Reiner Holzemer

Auguste, 50 years old, from Heppenheim, on the 1938 rally

“If I just tell you the plain facts, you won’t be able to visualise what it was like. The atmosphere, the enthusiasm radiated by the crowds of people. Young and old, Austrians, Sudeten Germans, people from all over the Reich, stood side by side, all waiting with the same patience.”

Letter 1938
Dokumentationszentrum Reichsparteitagsgelände

Theodor, 59 years old, Mayor of the city of Essen, on the 1935 rally

"Simply tremendous. We've put America in the shade. […] He aims to build for millennia, that is his plan."

Diary entry 1935
Stadtarchiv Essen 652 Nr. 140, 149

Charlotte, 19 years old, from Nuremberg, on the 1933 rally

"The parade ground of the 100,000 was an absolute dump. Cigarette packets, chocolate bar wrappers, broken bottles, rags etc. Piles of rubbish were swept together and ceremoniously burned."

Report 1933
Dokumentationszentrum Reichsparteitagsgelände

Emil, 14 years old, from Nuremberg, on the 1934 rally

"As I already wrote, I helped out at the inn. [...] The inn was overcrowded; [...] Although we'd slaughtered a big sow in advance, we ran out of our homemade sausages. My mother and father were so busy that although Hitler often passed by in our, or in the neighbouring street, they didn't see him."

Record book 1934
Stadtarchiv Nürnberg E1_2214_2_01

Reinhold, 17 years old, from Bonn,
member of the Reich Labour Service, on the 1937 rally

"How we had to line up, enter the field etc., was all fixed meticulously in advance. And I [...] would have cried if I hadn't been allowed to go along."

Contemporary witness interview 1997
Dokumentationszentrum Reichsparteitagsgelände/Reiner Holzemer

"City of the Nazi Party Rallies"

In 1933 Hitler chose Nuremberg as the venue for all future Nazi Party Rallies. The town council assumed an active role as host and dedicated huge financial and human resources to the mass events.

Mayor Liebel marketed the city intensively under the label *City of the Nazi Party Rallies*. In order to create the desired traditional German backdrop for the rallies, any *disfiguring elements* were removed. Begun in 1933, the construction measures were not aimed at conservation and reconstruction, but at the invention of a fake tradition stretching back from the *Third Reich* to the medieval empire [Kaiserreich].

Based on their conception of the city as a central propaganda venue, local protagonists claimed for Nuremberg a role model function in the *Jewish Question:* boycotts, the demolition of the main synagogue and expropriation of Jewish property were particularly early and drastic measures.

Nuremberg as "International Tourist Magnet"

The number of overnight stays in Nuremberg rose significantly between 1933 and 1938. There was hardly a sector that did not hope to benefit economically from the rallies. In particular, trade in all manner of souvenirs thrived. Besides postcards of famous sights, the special beer mugs emblazoned with the city coat of arms were exceptionally popular. Souvenirs such as pencil cases in the city colours and with a dedication by the mayor were produced.

← Postcard *Nuremberg, City of the Nazi Party Rallies*, 1933
Dokumentationszentrum Reichsparteitagsgelände D-0334-01

↙ Decorated city gate *Welcome to the City of the Nazi Party Rallies* 1937
Stadtarchiv Nürnberg A76-RF_294_3_1

→ Beer tankards *Nuremberg, City of the Nazi Party Rallies* 1930s
Dokumentationszentrum Reichsparteitagsgelände DZO-0008/
exhibit photography: Tim Hufnagl

Nürnberg
die Stadt der
Reichsparteitage

Besucht den
einzigartigen, stimmungsvollen und historische
Nürnberger Christkindlesmark
auf dem Adolf Hitlerplatz vom 4. bis 24. Dezembe
Lith. Kunstanst
LEONH. AMERSDORF
NÜRNBERG

Christmas Market and "Christmas Boycott"

In 1933 Mayor Liebel moved the Christmas Market to the main market square, establishing the tradition of the opening ceremony with a live "Christ Child" and elaborate Christmas lights that is still upheld today. During the festive season Gauleiter Streicher also encouraged local *Christmas boycotts* aimed at spoiling the Christmas business of Jewish retailers.

← Poster *Nuremberg Christmas Market* 1933
Stadtarchiv Nürnberg A 28-1933_0002

→ Fränkische Tageszeitung 17.12.1937
Stadtbibliothek Nürnberg Ztg 00113 (1937, 11–12)

Freitag, 17. Dezember 1937 — Fränkische Tageszeitung

Kein Deutscher kauft beim Juden!

Nürnberg im Zeichen des Boykotts der jüdischen Geschäfte

Demolition of the Synagogue

Referring to the *Regulations for the New Design of German Cities [Gesetz über die Neugestaltung deutscher Städte]*, Mayor Liebel and Gauleiter Streicher were able to have the main synagogue demolished even before the *Night of Broken Glass* on 9 November 1938. Coinciding with the beginning of the Nazi Party Rally in September 1938, Streicher's *Fränkische Tageszeitung* reported on the *erasing of the last eyesore.*

↑ Streicher (right) and Liebel (left) 1938
Dokumentationszentrum Reichsparteitagsgelände D-0164-03

Fake Tradition

Marking the 1937 rally, in cooperation with the city and party, the German National Museum mounted the exhibition entitled *From the City of the Imperial Diets to the City of the Nazi Party Rallies [Von der Stadt der Reichstage zur Stadt der Reichsparteitage]*. Nuremberg was stylised as the crystallisation pointof Greater Germany's imperial history in the Middle Ages.

↑ Exhibition poster *Nuremberg, The German City* 1937
Stadtarchiv Nürnberg A 28-1937_0002_1

Willy Liebel in a city council meeting 1933

"A new era has dawned in Germany."

↗ Stadtarchiv Nürnberg C 7/IX Nr. 534
↓ Willy Liebel 1940, Stadtarchiv Nürnberg A 58_0123_LiebelWilli_OBM_17Jan1940

Preis: 20 Pfennig
Litauen und Memelgebiet 20 Pfennig
Übriges Ausland: 30 Pfennig

JB Illustrierter Beobachter

10. JAHRGANG / FOLGE 38 / DONNERSTAG, 19. SEPTEMBER 1935

VERLAG FRANZ EHER NACHF. G.M.B.H. MÜNCHEN 2 NO

„Das deutsche Reichsschwert dem Führer aller Deutschen!"

Bei der Eröffnung des Parteitages der Freiheit überreicht der Oberbürgermeister von Nürnberg dem Führer als symbolische Gabe eine wertvolle Nachbildung des alten Reichsschwertes.

Sonderaufnahme für den „J. B." von Heinrich Hoffmann.

Willy Liebel
1897–1945

As an early protagonist of the völkisch scene in Nuremberg, Willy Liebel put his printing business at its service. Streicher's *Stürmer* was also printed there. From 1929 onwards, he held a seat on the council for the Nazi Party. The unlawful composition of the town council in line with the Reichstag election results meant that Liebel was voted in as the new mayor of the *City of the Nazi Party Rallies* in April 1933.

Liebel specifically promoted Nuremberg's image as the *most German of all German cities*. Much of the so-called *purification [Entschandelung]* of the old town can be ascribed to him personally. From 1942 onwards, Liebel also worked for Albert Speer in the Ministry of Armaments. Liebel was found dead in Nuremberg at the end of the war in 1945.

Symbolic Politics

At the 1935 rally, in a gesture steeped with symbolism, Liebel presented Hitler as *heir of the German Emperors* with a replica of the imperial sword. In 1938, he instigated the return of the original imperial insignia from Vienna to Nuremberg.

← Liebel (left) and Hitler (right) 1935
in: Illustrierter Beobachter 19.9.1935, Dokumentationszentrum Reichsparteitagsgelände D-0326-02

Eva Rößner in an interview 2008

“After these events, who could say they hadn't known anything.”

↗ Helmut Reister: Nürnbergerin (82): „So erlebte ich die Reichskristallnacht“, in: Abendzeitung München 27.10.2008
↓ Eva Rößner 1942, property of Ursula Rössner

Staunch Witness of the Past
No easy matter for Eva Rößner: until her ninetieth year she talked about her memories of the Nazi period on countless occasions, answering the questions of school classes with endless patience.

↑ Eva Rößner in a contemporary-witness interview 2013
Dokumentationszentrum Reichsparteitagsgelände D-0323-01

Eva Rößner
1926–2019

Directly after the seizure of power, Eva Rößner's family from Nuremberg fell victim to political and racial persecution. Her father Walter Jakob came from a well-to-do Jewish merchant family. Along with Eva's mother Gretl, he was active in the socialist workers' movement.

In March 1933, her father went into hiding and emigrated. Following the arrest of her mother immediately afterwards, the non-Jewish grandparents looked after the children. Walter Jakob effected his wife's release by divorcing her, but the family remained under Gestapo surveillance. Until the last, they stayed in contact with their Jewish grandparents Max and Therese Jakob, who were deported to Izbica in 1942 and murdered. Eva and her brother Hans survived with their maternal *Ayran* family in Nuremberg.

Precious shards

Memories of the destruction in the Night of Broken Glass in November 1938 ran particularly deep and were indelible. Eva Rößner described the home of her Jewish grandparents as a chaotic scene of wreckage, with everything destroyed. After Eva Rößner's death, her daughter gave the Documentation Centre a unique exhibit – the shards of a crystal vase destroyed on that night.

↓ Shards of the Jakob family's vase 9.11.1938
Dokumentationszentrum Reichsparteitagsgelände DZO-0163/
exhibit photography: Tim Hufnagl

Rally Grounds Building Site

Vision of a “Gesamtkunstwerk”

Buildings had a special significance for Hitler. The Nazi Party Grounds were to form the architectural backdrop for the staging of the social and political order of the Third Reich. With his plans for Nuremberg, architect Albert Speer aspired to hitherto unprecedented dimensions.

The building project was realised by the Special-Purpose Association Nazi Party Rallies Nuremberg [Zweckverband Reichsparteitag Nürnberg], founded specifically for the purpose and funded by the German Reich. The city contributed land and parts of its administrative apparatus. In 1938, the estimated building costs were in the region of 600 million reichsmarks – and rising.

Far beyond their architectural function, as part of the propaganda, models of the buildings were designed to prefigure a vision of the rally grounds as a *Gesamtkunstwerk*. At the beginning of the war, construction was largely halted. Only two buildings were completed.

“Greatest Builder of All Time”

The propaganda narrative styled Hitler as an approachable visionary of the New Germany and its architecture.

→ Drawing of Hitler on the building site 1939
in: Berliner Illustrierte Zeitung 20.4.1939, Dokumentationszentrum Reichsparteitagsgelände D-0326-01

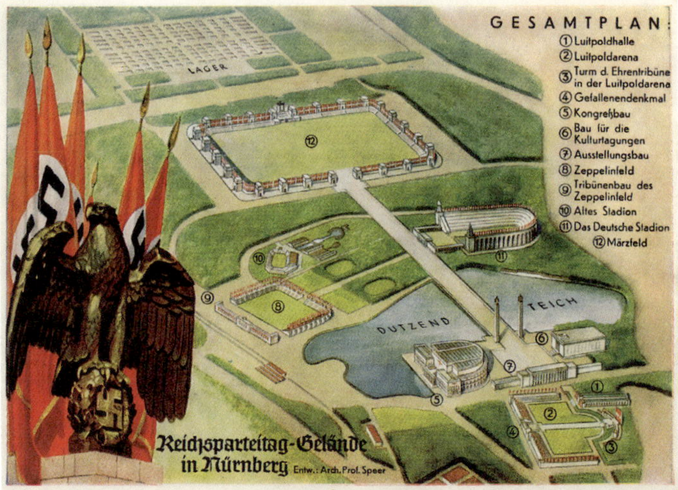

Blueprint for Utopia

Of the overall plan for the rally grounds, only Luitpold Arena and Zeppelin Field had been completed by the beginning of the war. The landscape plans envisaged an area solely for the rallies with no use for leisure activities.

↑ Postcard with overall map of the grounds 1937
Dokumentationszentrum Reichsparteitagsgelände Ph-1167

Rally Grounds Building Site

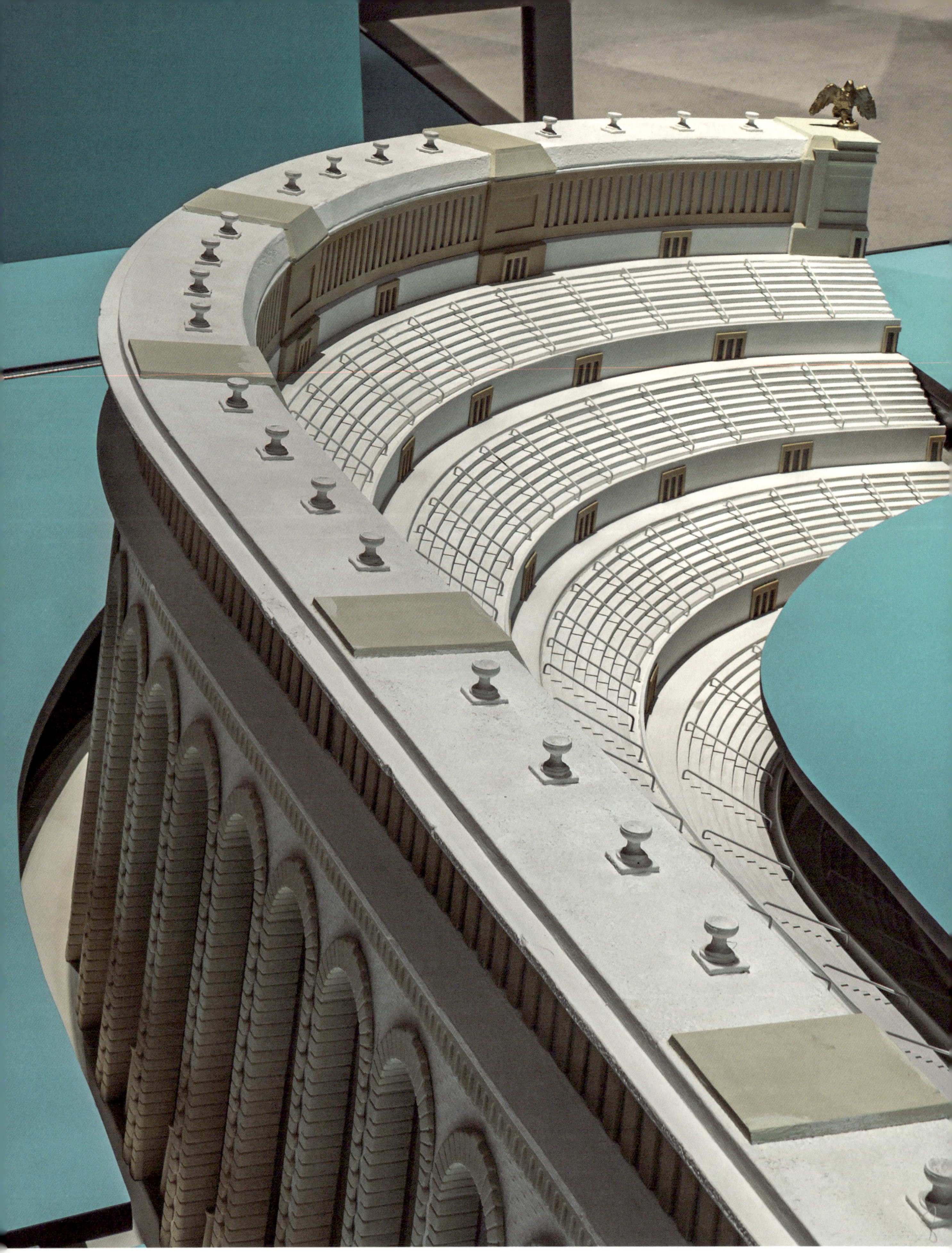

International Model Exhibition

Work on the German Stadium had not progressed beyond the excavation of the foundation pit when construction was halted in 1939. A large-scale model was presented at the laying of the foundation stone in 1937 and toured Europe from 1940 to 1943 as part of the *New German Architecture [Neue Deutsche Baukunst]* exhibition.

↑ Exhibition hall in Barcelona 1942
Arxiu Nacional de Catalunya 340717, 0029

Model Segment of the German Stadium

Large models on a scale of 1:100 played a major role in the Nazi propaganda. However, none of the original models have survived. In 2005, director Heinrich Breloer had a replica built for his film Speer and Hitler: The Devil's Architect [Speer und Er].

← Model segment of the German Stadium 2005
Dokumentationszentrum Reichsparteitagsgelande DZ-0164/
exhibit photography: Stefan Meyer

Attraction outside the Rallies

Guided tours of the building site, including the model exhibition, were offered several times daily.

↑ Poster advertising tours after 1935
Stadtarchiv Nürnberg C 32/I Nr. 41

↓ Ludwig Ruff 1920s, Stadtarchiv Nürnberg C 21/VII Nr. 132_Ruff, Ludwig_1

Ludwig Ruff
1878–1934

Based in Nuremberg since 1908, architect Ludwig Ruff initially embraced traditional architecture. Seeking a new style, at the end of the 1920s he combined modern forms with traditional architectural styles and monumentality. In 1931 he proposed erecting a guildhall on the Dutzendteich lakeside.

This project thus made him the obvious choice for the design of the Congress Hall in the same place. Allegedly an idea of Hitler, the project was the first of the monumental buildings of the Nazi regime. Ruff died unexpectedly in 1934. His son Franz took over the architect's office and all current commissions, including the Congress Hall, until work stopped after the war began.

Phoebus Palace

The Phoebus Palace cinema, opened in 1927 and designed by Ruff, displayed a mix of modern ribbon windows and traditional arches. Theatre buildings and film sets were considered important precursors of monumental architecture dating from 1933.

← Phoebus-Palast Nuremberg 1927
in: Fränkische Monatshefte 5 (1928), Dokumentationszentrum Reichsparteitagsgelände D-0302-03

Albert Speer in a meeting 1942

"The SS and police should take a hard line and put known slackers in work camps. It's the only way."

↗ Bundesarchiv Berlin R 3 Nr. 1697
↓ Albert Speer 1938, in: Die Woche 24.8.1938, Dokumentationszentrum Reichsparteitagsgelände D-0320-02

Albert Speer
1905–1981

In 1933, Albert Speer became Germany's leading architect and in 1934 was commissioned to design an overall plan of the Nazi Party Rally Grounds. As *General Building Inspector for the Reich Capital [Generalbauinspektor für die Reichshauptstadt]*, Speer was the key player in the German construction industry. As an architect, he had already employed criminal methods, by approving 13 million reichsmarks for the extension of Ausschwitz-Birkenau concentration camp.

In his capacity as armaments minister, from 1942 onwards, he was among those mainly responsible for the use of forced labour. Nevertheless, Speer was only sentenced to 20 years imprisonment at the *Nuremberg Trial*. In 1966, he launched a third career in the Federal Republic of Germany as a best-selling author and prominent contemporary witness of Nazism.

Regular Building Site Visits
Up to 1939, Hitler frequently staged himself with his favourite architect on the building site, here inspecting progress in Nuremberg.

← Speer (right), Hitler (left) and Liebel 1935
Bayerische Staatsbibliothek München/Bildarchiv, Fotoarchiv Hoffmann J.88

Architecture as Backdrop

To achieve the desired effect at the rallies, the architecture was elaborately highlighted by light, fire and flags. The illumination of the Zeppelin Grandstand at the so-called *Cathedral of Light [Lichtdom]* enhanced the religious character of the staging. Two large fire bowls and several floodlights were envisaged in the plans.

Even before 1933, the Nazi Party celebrated a veritable cult of the flag at its events. Flags assumed key importance at the rallies. Swastika flags were used to adorn the architectural backdrop and for the staging of the uniformed masses. Their highly prominent presence symbolised power.

New loudspeaker technology projected the speeches on to the field, enabling almost simultaneous commands to control the mass choreography.

Cult of the Flag

Technically perfected, the flag cult created spectacular images for contemporary observers. Huge flags were an integral part of the decoration of rally buildings, underscoring their solemn atmosphere.

↑ Luitpold Hall 1938
Dokumentationszentrum Reichsparteitagsgelände D-0314-04

↗ Luitpold Arena 1938
Dokumentationszentrum Reichsparteitagsgelände D-0314-03

"Cathedral of Light"

Hundreds of different types of floodlights were used for the staging of Zeppelin Field and Zeppelin Grandstand. As the climax of the Roll Call of the Political Leaders [Appell der Politischen Leiter], Albert Speer positioned anti-aircraft lights around the field whose light beams shot far into the sky. So impressive for the time, it prompted artist Robert Sluka to paint the *Cathedral of Light* in 1938. Countless photographs attempted to capture the spectacle.

← Floodlight to illuminate the Zeppelin Grandstand around 1936
Dokumentationszentrum Reichsparteitagsgelände DZO-0165/
exhibit photography: Christian Sperber

↙ Robert Sluka: *Nürnberg 9. Sept. 1938*
Dokumentationszentrum Reichsparteitagsgelände DZO-0141/
exhibit photography: Rudi Ott

↓ *Cathedral of Light* on the Zeppelin Field 1936
Dokumentationszentrum Reichsparteitagsgelände Ph-0731-02

Granite from Concentration Camps

Albert Speer needed large quantities of natural stone for his building projects. Granite was a preferred material for his monumental architecture. In 1937, Speer sought the cooperation of the SS in order to reduce costs. He funded the German Earth and Stone Works [Deutsche Erd- und Steinwerke (DESt)], an SS enterprise. By setting up concentration camps close to quarries, DESt was to supply granite for the buildings on the rally grounds and other Speer projects.

While *German Labour* was glorified with tens of thousands of Reich Labour Service men at the 1938 rally, countless prisoners slaved in concentration camp quarries. Physical toil, a lack of safety measures, hunger, cold and the brutality of the SS caused the death of thousands of prisoners in concentration camp quarries.

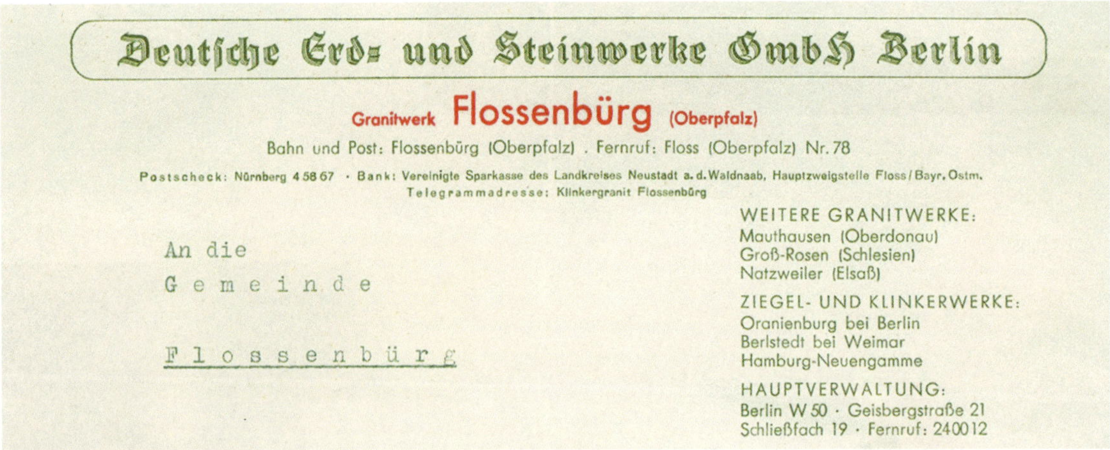
Deutsche Erd- und Steinwerke GmbH Berlin

Granitwerk Flossenbürg (Oberpfalz)

Bahn und Post: Flossenbürg (Oberpfalz) . Fernruf: Floss (Oberpfalz) Nr. 78

Postscheck: Nürnberg 4 58 67 · Bank: Vereinigte Sparkasse des Landkreises Neustadt a. d. Waldnaab, Hauptzweigstelle Floss/Bayr. Ostm.
Telegrammadresse: Klinkergranit Flossenbürg

An die
G e m e i n d e

F l o s s e n b ü r g

WEITERE GRANITWERKE:
Mauthausen (Oberdonau)
Groß-Rosen (Schlesien)
Natzweiler (Elsaß)

ZIEGEL- UND KLINKERWERKE:
Oranienburg bei Berlin
Berlstedt bei Weimar
Hamburg-Neuengamme

HAUPTVERWALTUNG:
Berlin W 50 · Geisbergstraße 21
Schließfach 19 · Fernruf: 240012

German Earth and Stone Works

The German Earth and Stone Works company organised the exploitation of prisoners in the quarries of Flossenbürg, Mauthausen, Groß-Rosen and Natzweiler-Struthof concentration camps. Natzweiler-Struthof concentration camp was set up specifically for the planned German Stadium.

↑ Letterhead DESt 1943
KZ-Gedenkstätte Flossenbürg

Quarry Work

The DESt also attempted to produce high quality stones in the concentration camps by training prisoners. Success was limited – due in part to the arbitrary brutality in the concentration camp system.

↓ Flossenbürg concentration camp quarry around 1942
Instituut voor Oorlogs-, Holocaust- en Genocidestudies, Amsterdam 67105

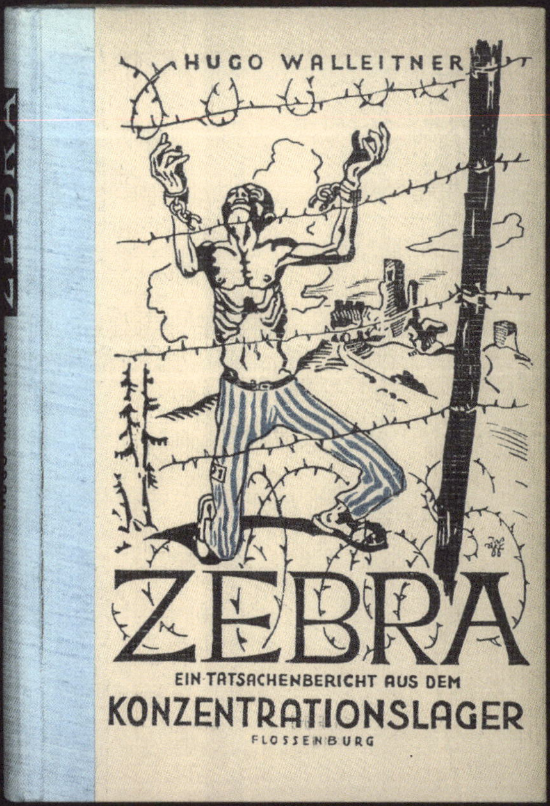

Worked to Death

After the war, many prisoners dealt with their traumatic experiences in concentration camps in books and drawings.

↑ Richard Grune: *Gefangener im Steinbruch* 1947
in: Passion des 20. Jahrhunderts, Hamburg 1947

↗ Hugo Walleitner: Zebra. Ein Tatsachenbericht aus dem Konzentrationslager Flossenbürg, Bad Ischl 1946
Dokumentationszentrum Reichsparteitagsgelände DZO-0166

Sergij Rybalka in an interview 2000

“No one here was sorry for any of us prisoners. [...] Many were killed or injured by falling stones.”

↗ Dokumentationszentrum Reichsparteitagsgelände
↓ Sergij Rybalka 2000, Dokumentationszentrum Reichsparteitagsgelände Ph-1044

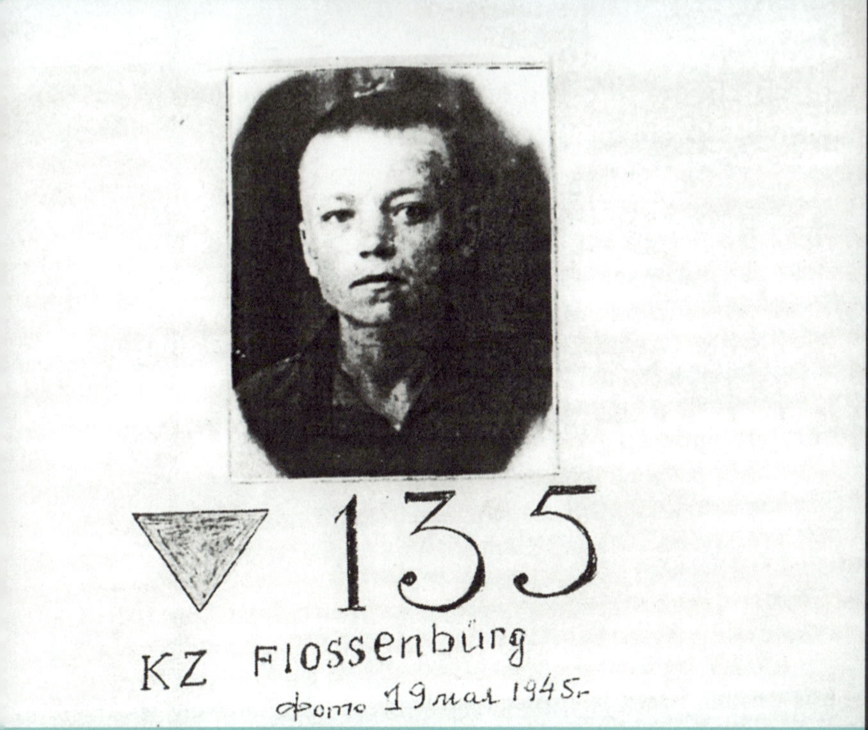

Prisoner Number 135

Sergij Rybalka after liberation in 1945. Under his photo he drew the prisoner symbol and low prisoner number of 135. The number of a dead prisoner, he was assigned to by the SS in 1942.

↑ Inscribed photo of Sergij Rybalka 1945
Archiv der Arbeitsgemeinschaft ehemaliges KZ Flossenbürg e.V.

Sergij Rybalka
1925–2013

Sergij Rybalka was deported in 1942 from the Ukraine to Germany as a forced labourer. After a failed escape attempt, the Gestapo sent him to Flossenbürg concentration camp in 1942. Initially, he was set to work in the granite quarry. The prisoners knew that stone from Flossenbürg was also destined for Nuremberg.

On 23 April 1945 the US Army liberated Sergij Rybalka and other sick prisoners left at the camp. He returned to the Ukraine and resumed work as an engineer in his home town of Poltawa, where he is chairman of an anti-Fascist resistance fighters' organisation. Sergij Rybalka comes to Germany regularly and was interviewed by the Documentaion Centre Nazi Party Rally Grounds as a contemporary witness.

Nazi Party Rally as Media Event

Posed Pictures – Implanted Memories

Nazi propagandists soon realised the suggestive impact of visual propaganda and deployed it to a hitherto unprecedented extent. The elevated status of Heinrich Hoffmann as Hitler's *personal photographer [Leibfotograf]* alone indicates the importance of images for the regime.

Moving pictures attracted even more attention than photographs. The newsreels in German cinemas initially reported the mass events in Nuremberg in a fairly unemotional tone. In the government-commissioned film production *Triumph of the Will [Triumph des Willens]*, director Leni Riefenstahl created powerful imagery to convey the ideal of the 1934 rally.

The sophisticated imagery was not a documentation of the real events. It glorified the *Nuremberg experience* and implanted selective memories. Along with the many souvenirs, it was intended to forge a long-lasting emotional bond to the community experience and thus to the Nazi state.

Scrapbooks, Commemorative Volumes, Badges

An unprecedented flood of pictures conveyed the rally experience to the public at large. Photos dominated the merchandising products as souvenirs of the rallies. Besides postcards and various commemorative volumes, scrapbooks were among the most popular products. Runs of millions were printed. Rally badges were top sellers.

← Rally badges 1934, 1935, 1937, 1938
Dokumentationszentrum Reichsparteitagsgelände DZO-0011/
exhibit photography: Rudi Ott

↗ Display case with Scrapbooks for cigarette packet stickers and Souvenir postcards (partly replicas)
Dokumentationszentrum Reichsparteitagsgelände DZO-0171-01; -02/
exhibit photography: Christian Sperber

Adolf Hitler
BILDER-GRUPPE 29

Absent, but in the Picture

Most Germans did not attend the rallies. Extensive reporting, during and after the event, let them share the experience. Up to 750 journalists from Germany and abroad were accredited in Nuremberg. Many special editions and supplements on the rallies were published in daily and weekly newspapers. Reporting was subject to official instructions and widespread self-censorship.

Propaganda minister Joseph Goebbels used the *Greater German Broadcasting Corporation [Großdeutschen Rundfunk]* and inexpensive radios to ensure a live experience of the rallies everywhere and to reach a wide audience. Television was launched in March 1935. However, the envisaged on-screen experience of the 1936 Nazi Party Rally failed not only due to the inexperience of the reporters: the fledgling technology of the new medium was unsuitable for propaganda purposes.

Rally on the radio

At the end of the 1930s, there were more than eleven million radios in Germany. They fell far short of reaching the entire population. Communal radio listening at the workplace, in pubs and apartment blocks was customary, especially during the rallies, and was promoted intensively by Nazi propaganda. Sometimes, the radio failed to work properly:

"We sat in our seats in the conference hall and listened to a garbled cacophony of shouting and noise over the loudspeaker for a solid one and half hours. Now and again, we caught a snippet or two from the mouth of the great ranter. It really put your nerves to the test. […] Suddenly, a young bookkeeper, who couldn't stand it any longer, burst into a fit of laughter. It was eerie listening to it. He cried with laughter, fell to the floor."

Excerpts from the autobiography of Josepha von Koskull (1898–1996) from Berlin, referring to a radio broadcast from the 1938 rally
in: Josepha von Koskull: Reichsparteitag der NSDAP 1938, Deutsches Historisches Museum-Bestand Inv.-Nr.: Do2 98/501

← Poster, Become a radio listener! n.y.
Stadtarchiv Bremen 9,P_03080

→ People's receiver type VE 301 GW
Dokumentationszentrum Reichsparteitagsgelände DZO-0168/
exhibit photography: Tim Hufnagl

60 50 40 30 20
VE 301
K
L

Wie Nürnberg rüstet

Die ungeheuren Vorarbeiten zum Reichsparteitag

(Sonderinformation des „8 Uhr-Blattes")

Die Ehrengäste

Reichs- und Länderregierungen

Sonstige Ehrengäste

Vertreter der Wehrmacht und Reichsmarine

Die ältesten Parteigenossen auf dem Reichsparteitag

Die 26 Quartierbezirke in Nürnberg

Nürnberg wird Millionenstadt

Kleinigkeiten

Vom Reichsparteitag in Nürnberg

Special Rally Issues

Special issues of the party magazine *Illustrated Observer [Illustrierter Beobachter]* brought pictures and reports from the rallies to all corners of the Reich. The independent national and local press also printed special issues. Reports were generally mundane and repetitive. Newspapers in Nuremberg treated readers to detailed background reports.

↑ 8-Uhr-Blatt 24.8.1933
Stadtbibliothek Nürnberg Ztg 16 (1933, 7–9)

↗ Illustrierter Beobachter 9.9.1933
Dokumentationszentrum Reichsparteitagsgelände D-0326-03

"Triumph of the Will"

Out of 130,000 metres of film footage from the 1934 rally, director Leni Riefenstahl created the illusion of a perfect rally, while ignoring the actual sequence of events. Commissioned by the party, she exploited the technical possibilities to the full. With a budget of 300,000 reichsmarks, she worked with 16 camera teams and a film crew of more than 100 strong. The official rally film was shown in German cinemas at the beginning of 1935.

→ Film poster *Triumph des Willens* 1935
Dokumentationszentrum Reichsparteitagsgelände D-0063-02

Behind the Scenes

In a contemporary coffee table book, a kind of "Making of" *Triumph of the Will,* Leni Riefenstahl described the various, in some cases innovative, production techniques. With special camera settings and positions, such as the lift on a flagpole in Luitpold Arena, a pit in the speaker's podium or facing backwards towards or in the middle of a fleet of vehicles, she spectacularly staged events and people in tune with Nazi ideology. Riefenstahl's focus was experience, not documentation. Unconventional clips, light and sound effects rounded off the cinematic construct.

← ↙ → → Filming 1934
in: Leni Riefenstahl: Hinter den Kulissen des Reichsparteitag-Films, München 1935, Stadtbibliothek Nürnberg Amb. 4. 1883

Fundamentals of Image Propaganda

With his posed photographs and publications, Heinrich Hoffmann became *Hitler's attendant on his rise to power.* The calculated selection, studied choreographies, arranged picture compositions and deliberate use of perspective mark these images as constructs of Nazi propaganda.

Hitler on the Speaker's Podium in the Luitpold Arena, 1935 Rally

The photograph of Adolf Hitler on the speaker's podium in the Luitpold Arena at the 1937 rally is characterised by its arranged composition and purposive employment of perspective: light and shadow, architecture and expressive symbols are used to achieve a specific effect.

→ Cigaretten-Bilderdienst (Hg.): Adolf Hitler. Bilder aus dem Leben des Führers, Leipzig 1936 u. a. Dokumentationszentrum Reichsparteitagsgelände D-0358

① The large, bright area of the speaker's podium dominates the frame and draws attention to the impressive-looking, monumental architecture. The effect is enhanced by the darker, disparate background. A focal point is formed by the swastika on the light background in the centre of the frame.

② Compared to the small figure of Hitler, the buildings appear even more monumental. The perspective enhances Hitler's appearance by elevating him and setting him apart from the spectators. Thanks to the "idealised" spectator perspective and cropping of the shot, Hitler stands alone above the masses, clearly recognisable despite his small stature.

③ Standard bearers in the background intensify the contrast to Hitler. Etched against the bright sky, Hitler stands out in the foreground from the dark-backdropped, anonymous mass. The cropping and bright sky in the frame emphasise the eagle as the central Nazi symbol.

Hitler and Hess in the Luitpold Arena, 1937 Rally

This photograph of Adolf Hitler and Rudolf Hess in the Luitpold Arena at the 1937 rally is a good example of calculated choreography. Not only the position, bearing and line of gaze of the two figures, but also the surroundings, in particular the flags, were selected to convey the desired message.

→ Heinrich Hoffmann: Parteitag der Arbeit, Berlin 1937
Dokumentationszentrum Reichsparteitagsgelände D-0359

① Hitler is clearly leading the way, distancing himself from his companions. His body language and direct gaze into the camera create the impression of movement and cause viewers to focus on him.

② Compared to the others, Hess is much closer to Hitler. This marks him out as the *Führer's deputy*. His bearing and line of gaze intensify the sense of dynamic movement.

③ The steps and SS guard of honour create perspective depth in the frame. The tapering toward the rear accentuates Hitler's central position.

④ The flags represent the pomp of the rallies. They occupy the top half of the image, dwarfing all the people in the frame. The central flag enhances the central perspective on Hitler.

⑤ Four media representatives – a photo journalist, two cameramen (one immediately above the entrance, the other on the flagpole lift), and the photographer are perfectly fitted into the composition and reveal the elaborate nature of the image production.

Leni Riefenstahl in an interview 1993

“So where, then, is my guilt?”

↗ Ray Müller: Die Macht der Bilder 1993
↓ Leni Riefenstahl 1934, in: Leni Riefenstahl: Hinter den Kulissen des Reichsparteitag-Films, München 1935, Stadtbibliothek Nürnberg Amb. 4. 1883

Leni Riefenstahl

1902–2003

Born and raised in Berlin, the trained dancer Leni Riefenstahl became involved in the film industry in 1925. Even prior to 1933, she had achieved success as an actress and director. A brief film about the 1933 rally, commissioned by the Nazi Party, was followed by *Triumph of the Will [Triumph des Willens]*. Winner of international awards, the film of the 1934 rally is still regarded as one of the most known propaganda films ever made.

Never a party member, after the war Riefenstahl was classed as a follower and was not convicted. She continued to work as a photographer and shot her first underwater film aged almost a hundred. Up to her death in 2003, Riefenstahl vehemently denied any political responsibility or moral guilt.

“The Power of Images”

To mark her 90th birthday, the filmmaker Ray Müller made Leni Riefenstahl the subject of a three-hour documentary in which she is confronted with her former filming location, the rally grounds. In 1993, he received an Emmy Award for his successful portrayal.

← Leni Riefenstahl on the Zeppelin Grandstand 1993
in: Ray Müller: Die Macht der Bilder 1993

Heinrich Hoffmann in an interview after 1945

"The photographer takes a picture. He captures the moment, nothing else."

↗ Tim Hoesmann: Hitler-Fotografien: Vom Recht an den Bildern des Bösen, in: Legal Tribune Online 14.2.2011
↓ Heinrich Hoffmann 1938, Bayerische Staatsbibliothek/Bildarchiv, Fotoarchiv Hoffmann M.86

Heinrich Hoffmann

1885–1957

Heinrich Hoffmann joined the Nazi Party early in 1920. As official *Reich photojournalist [Reichsbildberichterstatter]* he enjoyed exclusive access to Adolf Hitler. Between 1923 and 1945 the Munich photographer and his team took around half a million photos. With his monopoly on publication, he earned sums in the doubledigit millions with the *Hitler* brand.

At the end of the war he changed sides, identifying people on his pictures for the International Military Tribunal. He successfully defended himself against classification as a major war criminal during his *denazification*. He was released from prison in 1950 having served only fours years. His case was closed at the beginning of 1957.

"Inventor of the Leader Cult"

Hoffmann's *National Socialist Pictures Publishing House [Verlag nationalsozialistischer Bilder]* brought out almost twenty volumes with Hitler on the cover between 1933 and 1942. The close cooperation between Adolf Hitler and the photographer was a vital component of Hitler's self-staging.

← Heinrich Hoffmann: Hitler wie ihn keiner kennt, Berlin 1932
Dokumentationszentrum Reichsparteitagsgelände D-0327-01

International Reactions

The presence of foreign guests of honour and diplomats at the rallies was intended to boost Nazi Germany's international standing. Many hesitated to do Germany this honour. From 1935, in his official capacity as Reich Chancellor, Hitler therefore specifically invited foreign diplomats. Nevertheless, Great Britain and France did not send ambassadors until 1937. One year later, the US representative also attended, while the Soviet Union again declined the invitation.

Despite massive attempts to influence them, international journalists exposed the rallies as propaganda shows from the outset. Depending on the country, political leanings of the newspaper and time of publication, reporting was either critical or congratulatory. Proclamations of peaceful intentions in particular were met with scepticism in caricatures and articles.

André François-Poncet, Ambassador in Berlin, on the Nazi Party Rally 1937

"This mood […] strongly impressed foreign spectators. […] An effect is created that few can resist, they go back home, seduced and won over, willing to join in without realising the dangerous reality concealed by the deceptive pageantry of the magnificent marches."

in: André François-Poncet: Botschafter in Berlin, Mainz 1948, S. 273

Hitler in warlike speech

A warning note in reports on the 1938 *Rally of Greater Germany.*

→ The Chicago Daily News 12.9.1938
Dokumentationszentrum Reichsparteitagsgelände D-0333-02

On the Grandstand

Along with colleagues from Great Britain, Brazil and Turkey, the French ambassador André François-Poncet (fourth from left) watched the combat games at the 1937 rally.

↑ Diplomats on the Zeppelin Grandstand 1937
ullstein bild/Scherl Mediennr. 00280475

YES

COURTN
IN CO
ON G

'Ring on P
Aid as Tw
Get

More

Places raid
state's attorn
cluded the fo
number of pa
725 West R
the second flo
226 South W
seventh floor,
men.
10 North We
second floor,
135 South W
third floor, 1
813 East 43d s
50 of them w
4721 Br
and 40 women.

The state adv
in its court wa
though 66 deten
want of sufficie
today's hearing
Street Court,
Courtney's offi
cases on the do
from last wee
which came up
continued on p
fendants' attorn
In addition,
volving a policy
"talked" was c
of the defense.
After today's
Clement Dernb
sistant in the
clared that he
winning a con

st Political Show on Earth"

k: "Congress of Freedom" Signalizes Germany's Rearmament; ational Flag; Jews Deprived of Citizenship; Lithuania Attacked

ddle
ling-
ufac-
,000

vhen
ve of
ation
they
stag
for
eries

ürer
dolf
week
hou-
nized
nany

on
the
redi-
rked

d for
umb-
imes
s of
sau-
5,000
offee,
was

ning
was
free-
was
ions.
with
neu-
dom
nter-

© Strube

The Boomerang

—*Strube in* The Daily Express *(London)*

Said Reichsleader Hitler: "The insult to the German flag—which has been settled in the most loyal manner by the American Government—is an illustration of the attitude of Jewry toward Germany, even when it is in an official capacity. . . ."

Apology

Hitler referred to Magistrate Louis B. Brodsky, of New York, who dismissed most of those arrested in the *Bremen* incident, at the same time comparing the swastika emblem to a pirate flag.

Secretary of State Cordell Hull apolo-

olic), and "certain elements of the stupid and reactionary bourgeoisie."

A sharp retort to Hitler's charge that the Catholic clergy of Germany was mingling in politics instead of looking exclusively to the care of souls was made by *L'Osservatore Romano*, the Vatican's official organ:

"The clergy's activity to-day is devoid of any political character. It is strictly connected with the defense of Catholic dogmatic and moral principles, as well as the spiritual welfare of the faithful."

Meanwhile, the German Embassy at Washington was formally notified on Sep-

The Boomerang
The caricature illustrates that anti-Semitic Nazi policies incurred economic sanctions for the German Reich.

← The Daily Express September 1935
Dokumentationszentrum Reichsparteitagsgelände D-0333-03

Singers Booed Off Stage
Booed by an international audience in the Soviet newspaper Isvestija: Hitler as hysterical tenor, Göring as brittle bass and Goebbels as a squealing rat.

↓ Isvestija 17.9.1936
Dokumentationszentrum Reichsparteitagsgelände D-0333-04

Unity Mitford in a letter to the "Stürmer" 1935

"We are looking forward to the day when we will be powerful enough to declare: England for the English!"

↗ Der Stürmer Nr. 30/1935
↓ Unity Mitford 1935, Stadtarchiv Nürnberg E 39 Nr. 2336_001

In topranking Nazi circles

At the 1937 rally Unity Mitford is seated directly behind the swimmer Anni Brandt, married to Hitler's doctor Karl Brandt, Hitler's lover Eva Braun and Heinrich Hoffmann's wife Erna (left to right).

↑ Unity Mitford, Anni Brandt, Eva Braun and Erna Hoffmann on the main square 1937
Bayerische Staatsbibliothek München/Bildarchiv, Fotoarchiv Hoffmann L.65

Unity Mitford
1914–1948

In London, the young British aristocrat Unity Mitford socialised in the intellectual liberal circles of the Rothschild and Churchill families. In 1934 she joined the British fascist party, *The British Union of fascists*. She moved to Munich, learned German and became a fanatical supporter of Hitler and the Nazi Party. From 1933 onwards, she attended the rallies in Nuremberg every year. Mitford became acquainted with Streicher, Hitler, Goebbels and Göring and was a favoured guest in Bayreuth, Nuremberg and Berlin.

The day Britain declared war on Germany, she shot herself in the head in the English Garden in Munich. Badly injured, Mitford returned to England, her vision of a British-German alliance shattered. Shortly after the end of the war, she died as a result of her attempted suicide.

William Shirer in his dairy 10.9.1934

"You have to experience the likes of it at close quarters to understand the fascination Hitler exercised on the people, to feel the dynamism he unleashed in his movement."

↗ William Shirer: Berliner Tagebuch, Leipzig 1995
↓ William Shirer around 1940, ullstein bild/Scherl Mediennr. 4.01741273 (1)

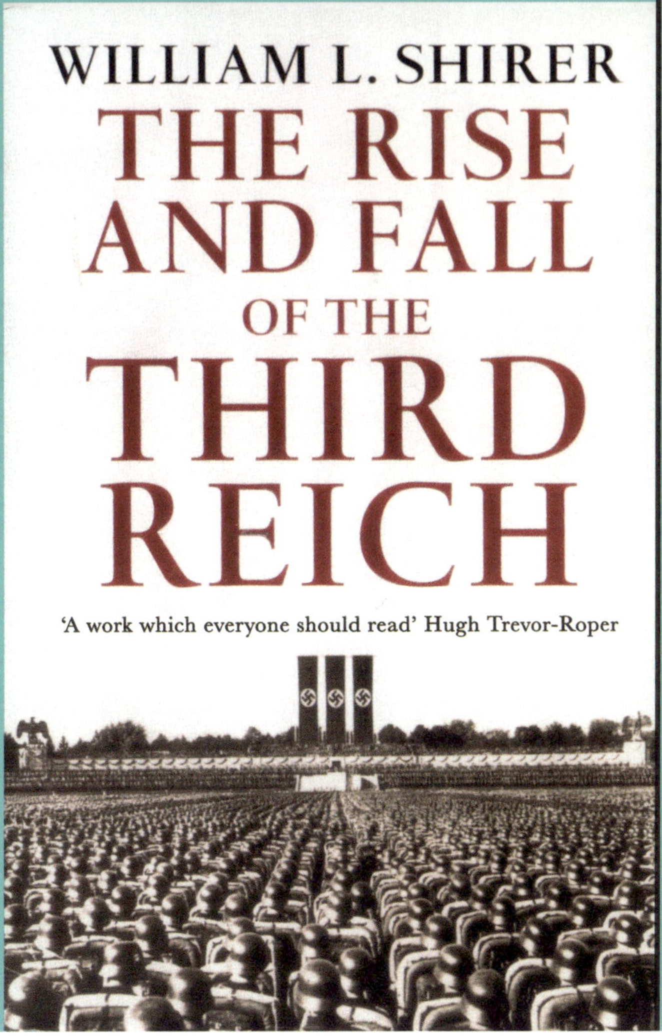

William Shirer
1904–1993

Aged 21, the American William Shirer took up the post of foreign correspondent for the *Chicago Tribune* in Paris in 1925. In summer 1934, he became the foreign correspondent of the news agency *Universal News Service* in Berlin and wrote about the rallies. In 1937 he moved to the fledgling medium of radio and reported regularly from Berlin and other European metropolises for *CBS New York.*

A history graduate, the journalist was present at the signing of the armistice with France in the Forest of Compiègne. Published in 1941 for the first time, his *Berlin Diary* enjoyed international success. At the end of the Second World War, he reported on the Nuremberg Trials. In 1947, he returned to the USA and reported on the founding of the United Nations.

Early Analysis

Based on original documents secured by the Allies, in 1960 William Shirer published a detailed historical analysis of the Nazi dictatorship entitled *Rise and Fall of the Third Reich.*

← William Shirer: The Rise and Fall of Adolf Hitler, London 1998
Dokumentationszentrum Reichsparteitagsgelände D-0332-01

Faces of Captivity

The living conditions and experiences of brutality for prisoners of war and forced labourers varied greatly. Behind every face is a fateful destiny.

→ Group of girls in a camp for East European forced labourers 1942
Stadtarchiv Nürnberg Bildchronik (Neg. N 208)

↘ Polish prisoners of war around 1940
Stadtarchiv Erlangen Rühl Negative 2461

1939 —45

OST

1939—45 The Rally Grounds in the War – Captivity, Forced Labour and Deportation

The rally grounds in September 1939: Germany's invasion of Poland unleashed the Second World War. Instead of cheering crowds, prisoners arrived in Nuremberg. The Wehrmacht turned the former camp for SA rally participants into a POW camp for 30,000 prisoners of war. The accessibility and infrastructure of the rally grounds provided the ideal prerequisites. Soldiers and officers of various nationalities were interned here until the end of the war. Their survival chances depended on their military rank, the course of the war and racial classification by the Nazis.

The grounds were not only attractive to the Wehrmacht. Private companies, the Gestapo and SS also set up camps there. In addition, they served as a hub from which *work details* of prisoners of war and civilian forced labourers were organised across northern Bavaria. Men and women from the occupied territories, soldiers and civilians alike, were used as forced labour, also in Nuremberg. They were an accustomed sight for Nuremberg's citizens.

Thousands of prisoners of war and forced labourers died during the war due to the catastrophic conditions or they were deliberately murdered. March Field [Märzfeld] station was to become the departure point for the deportation of more than 2000 Franconian Jews to the extermination camps. Very few survived.

Shoulder to shoulder
German workers and men in uniform, presumably Italian prisoners of war, working together in the Nuremberg Siemens factory. Prisoners of war and forced labourers were a common feature of life during the war.

← Forced labourers 1944
Siemens Historical Institute B 2805 TW

On the Way to the "Russian Camp"
The SA camp, which up to 1938 accommodated thousands of rally participants, was to become the so-called unofficial *Russian camp* with improvised tents to which Soviet prisoners of war marched four years later

↓ Prisoners of war 1942
Dokumentationszentrum Reichsparteitagsgelände Ph-0401-12

Rally Grounds Camp Complex

Captured Soldiers

By the end of 1939, 15,000 Polish soldiers had already been interned in the recently built main camp [Mannschafts-Stammlager-stalag] in Langwasser, Nuremberg. The prisoner of war camp was located in military district XIII. It was one of the largest in the Reich. Following the theatres of war, more than 150,000 soldiers from Western, Southern and Eastern Europe and the USA were interned at the camp through to 1945.

The manpower of the soldiers was an important resource for the German war economy. After a short time, most prisoners left the camp on *work details* in towns and in the country.

At the end of the war, the situation was catastrophic: thousands of soldiers and officers arrived at the camp, completely exhausted, only to be marched towards the heart of the Reich by the Wehrmacht. On liberating the camp on 17 April 1945, the US Army found 14,000 sick prisoners. Hundreds, mainly Soviet soldiers, died in the weeks that followed.

Self-assertion and Solidarity

Polish, French and Belgian prisoners of war secretly organised Olympic games at the stalag. Consisting of six disciplines, the events raised the spirits of the camp inmates. First place in the 50-metre race – completed in *frog jump* style – was won by Polish prisoner Teodor Niewiadomski. The prisoners modelled this discipline on a punishment popular with the German guards.

← Poster by E. Turbaczewski 1940
Muzeum Sportu i Turystyki w Warszawie
(Museum of Sports and Tourism in Warsaw) Nr. 3360

Wretched Living Conditions

After the liberation, investigator Bruce Macdonald inspected the former stalag in Langwasser. He was looking into violations of international law. *Exhibit S-3* documented the completely inadequate accommodation for the POWs during the last weeks of the war.

↑ Prisoner of war camp Nuremberg-Langwasser 1945
Windsor Public Library – Community Archives PC-6387

Improvisation and Cold

Polish prisoners of war waiting in front of the camp mess in sub-zero temperatures. In winter 1939/40 they lived in the former rally tents. They had to build the infrastructure of their imprisonment themselves – a barbed wire fence, watchtowers and barracks.

← Prisoner of war camp Nuremberg-Langwasser 1939
Stadtarchiv Erlangen Rühl-Negative 2466

On arrival, prisoners were subjected to an arduous and degrading registration process. The Belgian prisoner of war Pierre Fourage recorded his impressions of registration in Nuremberg-Langwasser in summer 1940.

Wednesday, 26th of June;
26th day of captivity

After breakfast at 6:45, we assemble and are taken to the notorious camp that is the subject of so much rumour. No one who was there has ever come back, and for good reason.
Immediately on arrival, we are put through a whole series of formalities. In groups of twenty, we enter a huge, official-looking tent.
Our particulars are noted and we are registered. This means that they hang a sign around our necks. We lose our identity and are now nothing but a number. From now on, I am prisoner 48007.
In the next office, we are robbed of our money, in exchange for a confirmation of receipt! Further up the line, we have to turn out our pockets. We are only allowed to keep our watches. Our particulars and details of our professions are taken again. In the next room, they take our photos, in the pose of a person sentenced to death, sign on chest.
And then comes the body search. They take away the last possessions we have.

Recordings von Pierre Fourage o.J.
CegeSoma (Studien- und Dokumentationszentrum für Krieg und zeitgenössische Gesellschaften) AB1575

André Vergnes in his notes 1945

"Dearest Mum, dear Father, what are you thinking about your son? I can't wait to see you again."

↗ Property of Marie-José Panarin/Bruno Vergnes
↓ André Vergnes around 1940, property of Marie-José Panarin/Bruno Vergnes

The Soup

Vergnes drew a key subject of captivity. Prisoners crowding around the soup pot. Rations often fell short of the prescribed amounts.

↑ André Vergnes: *La Soupe* 1940
Property of Marie-José Panarin/Bruno Vergnes

André Vergnes
1917–1967

André Marie Vergnes was born in the South of France. Called up at the age of 22, he was forced to curtail his art studies. In June 1940, he was captured and taken to the Langwasser stalag. At the time, it was full of prisoners of war from Belgium and France.

Vergnes only remained at the camp a short time before being sent on a work detail in the country. He drew and painted in his free time. Some of his pictures capture the situation in the stalag in summer 1940. After nearly five years' captivity, he returned to Paris in 1945 and became a high school art teacher.

Angelo Cottinelli in his will dated 24.6.1944

“To my young nephews, Vincenzino and Tonino, I leave my box of building bricks.”

↗ Property of Vincenzo Cottinelli
↓ Angelo Cottinelli 1943, property of Vincenzo Cottinelli

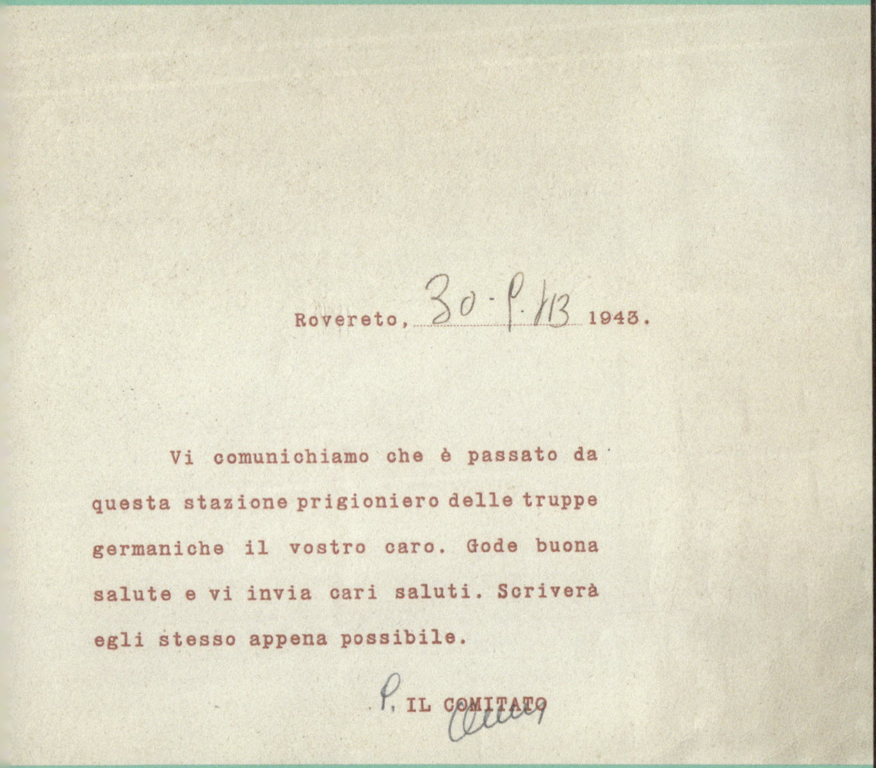

Rovereto, 30 · 9 · 43 1943.

Vi comunichiamo che è passato da questa stazione prigioniero delle truppe germaniche il vostro caro. Gode buona salute e vi invia cari saluti. Scriverà egli stesso appena possibile.

P. IL COMITATO

Signs of Life

A postcard from the Red Cross informed Angelo Cottinelli’s family that he had been taken prisoner, was in good health, sent his greetings and would get in touch soon.

↑ Postcard to Maria Cottinelli 1943
Property of Vincenzo Cottinelli

Angelo Cottinelli
1909–1944

Angelo Cottinelli was born in Brescia, Italy. Despite health issues, he was drafted in 1943. When, in September 1943, Italy signed an armistice with the Allies, he was taken prisoner. Already ill, he was deported as an Italian military internee (IMI) to the Langwasser stalag. The Nazi state denied IMIs protection under international law.

Angelo Cottinelli was dispatched on a *work detail.* His physical condition deteriorated sharply and he was committed to the hospital for prisoners of war in Langwasser. The order to send him back home came too late. He died on 25 June 1944, aged 34, in German captivity.

Eugene Murphy in his written reminiscences 1980s

“As prisoners of war we are fated to always be starving.”

↗ Property of Ryan Barr
↓ Eugene Murphy 1940s, pproperty of Ryan Barr

Eugene Murphy
1917–1988

Eugene Murphy was born in Illinois. On leaving school he worked in sales, joining the army at the end of 1940. Via Glasgow, the South of England and France, Eugene Murphy and his unit reached Luxembourg and Belgium at the end of October 1944. The last counter-attack by the Germans on the Western Front took their enemies by surprise with high losses on the US American side.

Eugene Murphy survived and was taken prisoner. He was deported to the Langwasser camp at Christmas 1944. The conditions there were chaotic at the time. He only stayed in Nuremberg for a few weeks and was liberated by US troops in southern Bavaria in April 1945. He returned to the USA in May and soon started a family.

A Prisoner’s View

An American prisoner of war managed to smuggle a camera into the camp: the photos show scenes of bomb craters, vermin and deprivation. After the war, the photos were circulated among the former prisoners, including Eugene Murphy, who stuck them in an album.

← Eugene Murphy’s photo album after 1945
Property of Ryan Barr

Officers: Prisoners and Eyewitnesses

In 1940, the Nazis once more planned a rally. The stalag was cleared in a hurry. However, the war dictated otherwise. There were no enthusiastic masses, just more prisoners, this time officers.

Officers fared better under international law and did not work. They were billeted in their own officer camps [oflags]. Thousands of men from France, Serbia, the Netherlands and from 1944 onwards, Italy, were interned here until 1945. They organised a culture and sports programme as a distraction from hunger, cold, cramped conditions and disease. Politicians and the Wehrmacht supported the cultural work. They wanted to prove that prisoners were well-treated.

Through the fence, the officers witnessed the misery of the Soviet prisoners in the unofficial *Russian camp*. Before liberation, the disastrous conditions in the stalag, brought back into use in 1943, were also to affect the officers.

Air Raids

A large part of the camp was destroyed by Allied air raids in 1943. In 1945, the camp hospital was damaged. The prisoners witnessed the bombing of Nuremberg with mixed feelings: hopes of an end to the war mingled with grief for those killed and satisfaction at the destruction.

↑ Bombed camp hospital 1945
Private property

Art in Captivity

↑Jean-Marie Cardine: *La lettre* 1941
Stadtarchiv Nürnberg E 1/2295 Nr. 1_17

↗ Giuseppe Tortorelli: View of Nuremberg from Langwasser prisoners camp 1944
Private property

→ Major van Weenen: *Symbol unserer Residenz in Nürnberg-Langwasser, das Kgf. Hemd, die Baracke, das Kohlfeld, der Barackenweg und der Stacheldraht* 1942
NIMH (Nederlands Instituut voor Militaire Historie) Den Haag

Document of Waiting

French officer Pierre Esch used every single millimetre of his diary. For months he recorded daily camp life and the activities with which he and fellow prisoners tried to bear life behind the barbed wire fence.

→ Pierre Esch's diary 1940 (replica)
Private property/exhibit photography: Tim Hufnagl

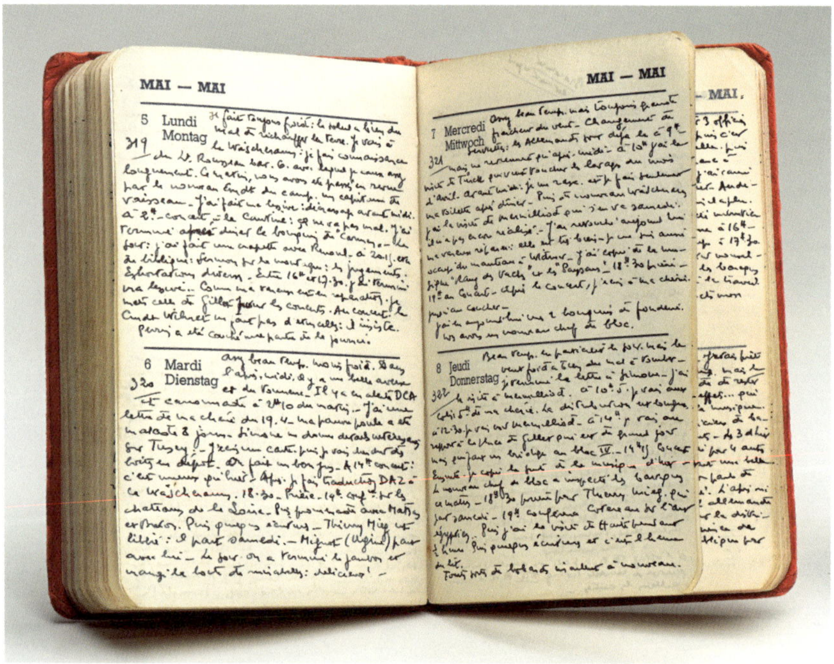

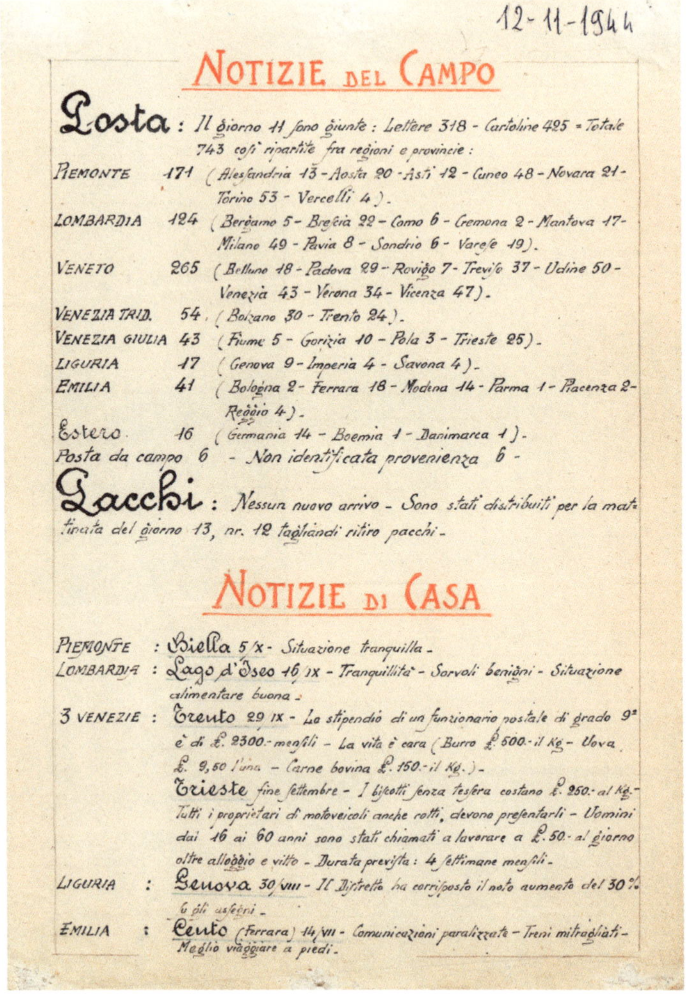

12-11-1944

NOTIZIE DEL CAMPO

Posta: Il giorno 11 sono giunte: Lettere 318 - Cartoline 425 = Totale 743 così ripartite fra regioni e provincie:

PIEMONTE 171 (Alessandria 13 - Aosta 20 - Asti 12 - Cuneo 48 - Novara 21 - Torino 53 - Vercelli 4).

LOMBARDIA 124 (Bergamo 5 - Brescia 22 - Como 6 - Gemona 2 - Mantova 17 - Milano 49 - Pavia 8 - Sondrio 6 - Varese 19).

VENETO 265 (Belluno 18 - Padova 29 - Rovigo 7 - Treviso 37 - Udine 50 - Venezia 43 - Verona 34 - Vicenza 47).

VENEZIA TRID. 54 (Bolzano 30 - Trento 24).

VENEZIA GIULIA 43 (Fiume 5 - Gorizia 10 - Pola 3 - Trieste 25).

LIGURIA 17 (Genova 9 - Imperia 4 - Savona 4).

EMILIA 41 (Bologna 2 - Ferrara 18 - Modena 14 - Parma 1 - Piacenza 2 - Reggio 4).

Estero 16 (Germania 14 - Boemia 1 - Danimarca 1).

Posta da campo 6 - Non identificata provenienza 6 -

Pacchi: Nessun nuovo arrivo - Sono stati distribuiti per la mattinata del giorno 13, nr. 12 tagliandi ritiro pacchi -

NOTIZIE DI CASA

PIEMONTE : Biella 5/X - Situazione tranquilla -

LOMBARDIA : Lago d'Iseo 16/IX - Tranquillità - Sorvoli benigni - Situazione alimentare buona -

3 VENEZIE : Trento 29/IX - Lo stipendio di un funzionario postale di grado 9° è di £. 2300.- mensili - La vita è cara (Burro £. 500.- il Kg - Uova £. 9,50 l'una - Carne bovina £. 150.- il Kg.) -

Trieste fine settembre - I biglietti senza tessera costano £. 250.- al Kg. - Tutti i proprietari di motoveicoli anche rotti, devono presentarli - Uomini dai 16 ai 60 anni sono stati chiamati a lavorare a £. 50.- al giorno oltre alloggio e vitto - Durata prevista: 4 settimane mensili -

LIGURIA : Genova 30/VIII - Il Distretto ha corrisposto il noto aumento del 30% ai gli ufficiali -

EMILIA : Cento (Ferrara) 14/VII - Comunicazioni paralizzate - Treni mitragliati - Meglio viaggiare a piedi -

Handwritten Camp Newspaper

The Italian officers brought out a camp newspaper between November 1944 and January 1945. The *Notizie del Campo [Camp News]* column provided information on the arrival of letters and parcels, while the *Notizie di Casa [Home News]* posted news from home.

← Camp newspaper 1944
A.N.E.I. Rom (Associazione Nazionale Ex Internati)

Zvi Asaria-Helfgott in his memoirs 1975

“Rumours spread that Jewish officers had to wear the yellow star of David.”

↗ Zvi Asaria-Helfgott: Wir sind Zeugen. Erlebnisbericht eines Juden aus deutschen Lagern. Niedersächsische Landeszentrale für Politische Bildung, Braunschweig 1975
↓ Hermann Helfgott um 1940, Yad Vashem Photo Archives 8546w44c

durch Austausch den Wünschen der Gefangenen nach französischer und italienischer Literatur entgegenzukommen. Ob an serbischen Dolmetschern ein ernstlicher Mangel besteht, kann nicht beurteilt werden, da die Zahl der Serben in diesem Lager nicht bekannt ist.

Über die Regelung der Verpflichtung zum Tragen des Judensterns durch Offiziere und Mannschaften jüdischer Rasse, über die auch in dem Bericht über das Lazarett Langwasser Klage geführt wird, bittet das A.A. um besondere Stellungnahme. Eine Benachteiligung der Juden bei der Verteilung von Paketen dürfte jedenfalls dann nicht zu rechtfertigen sein, wenn eine solche Benachteiligung dem vermutlichen Willen der Spender widerspricht. Der Delegierte bemerkt, daß im Oflag XIII B noch über 1000 Pakete des Roten Kreuzes auf ihre Verteilung warten. ~~Um eine besondere Mitteilung wird über die Regelung der Grußpflicht der gefangenen Offiziere und Unteroffiziere gegenüber deutschen Offizieren und Unteroffizieren gebeten.~~

In dem zum Oflag XIII B gehörigen Lazarett Langwasser fehlt es an Unterkleidung und

Zvi Asaria
1913–2002

Zvi Asaria was born in Yugoslavia as Hermann Helfgott to Jewish parents. He studied theology and, as a military cleric, ranked as an officer. He was captured by the Wehrmacht when the Balkans were overrun in 1941. Along with other Jewish prisoners, he was deported to the officers' camp in Langwasser.

Ignoring the ban on performing his duties as a cleric, he held clandestine services. He survived the Holocaust in German captivity, but his parents and siblings were brutally murdered in Yugoslavia. While still at the camp, the men learned of their families' fate. In 1948, he emigrated to Israel, took the name Zvi Asaria and worked as a rabbi. Until his death, he returned several times to Germany in this capacity.

Discrimination of Serbian Officers

The camp administration's order on wearing the *Star of David* caused a furore. An International Red Cross delegation forwarded the officers' complaint to its Geneva headquarters. In 1942, the order was repealed.

← Demand of February/March 1942
Politisches Archiv des Auswärtigen Amts RZ 405, 40976

Civilian Forced Labour

In late autumn 1941, as campaign successes stalled, labour shortages due to the war peaked. The Nazi regime decided to conduct mass deportations of foreign civilians to the Reich as forced labour, to supplement the prisoners of war. In 1942, thousands of men and women abducted from Eastern Europe reached March Field Station. The existing camp structure at Langwasser enabled a swift allocation of the new arrivals to workplaces.

A dense network of accommodation for forced labourers sprang up in Nuremberg. Strictly segregated according to racial criteria and country, people from Eastern Europe in particular had to endure abject living conditions. The Gestapo relied on deterrence and brutality in its surveillance and punishment of civilian forced labourers. In the work education camp on the grounds, terror similar to that of concentration camps prevailed.

A Nuremberg Example

Siemens rented accommodation throughout the city for its 7,500 forced labourers and prisoners from all over Europe. The Nuremberg factory also ran its own camp for *Eastern workers* and a satellite camp.

↑Siemens barracks for forced labourers in Katzwanger Straße 1944
Siemens Historical Institute B 2840 TW

“Russian Glade”

The reference R.W. for *Russenwiese* stands for the transfer of forced labourers to the work education camp of the Nuremberg-Fürth Gestapo. Inmates were subjected to weeks of terror and brutality to the point of death.

↓ Prison record book 1943
Staatsarchiv Nürnberg Polizeipräsidium Nbg.-Fürth Nr. 811

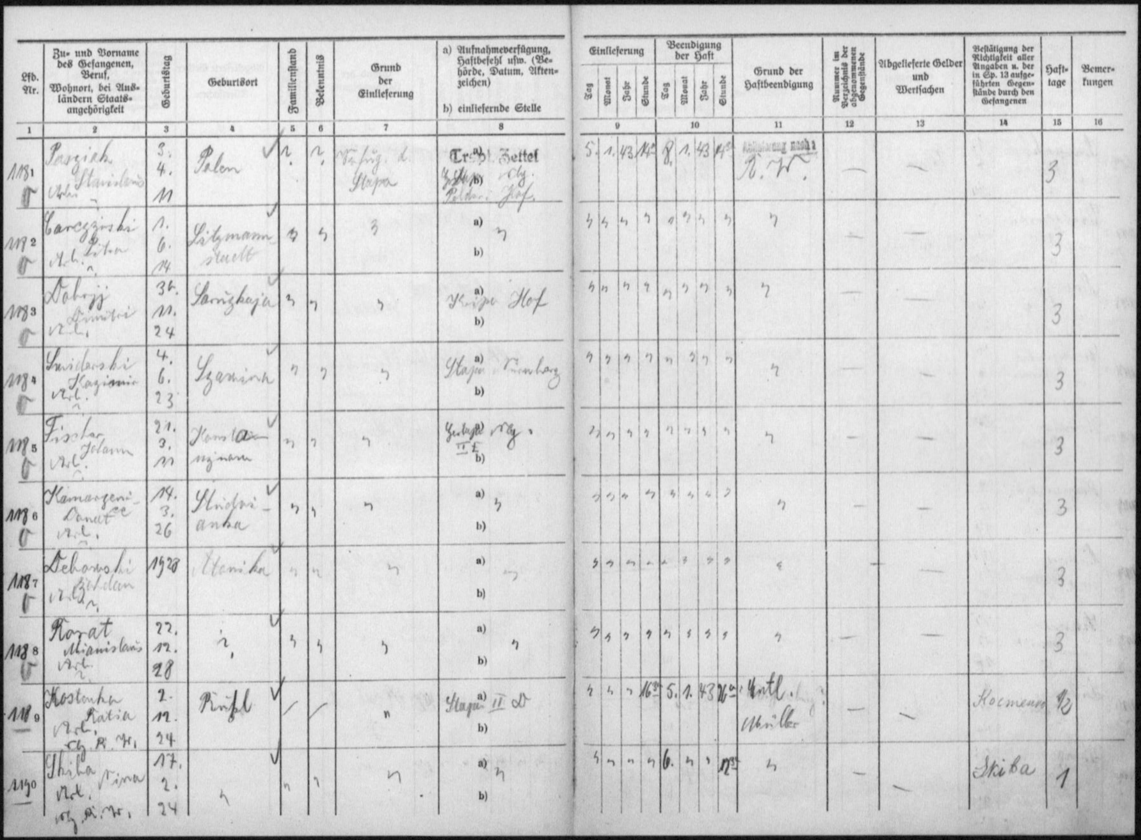

Lfd. Nr.	Zu- und Vorname des Gefangenen, Beruf, Wohnort, bei Ausländern Staatsangehörigkeit	Geburtstag	Geburtsort	Familienstand	Bekenntnis	Grund der Einlieferung	a) Aufnahmeverfügung, Haftbefehl usw. (Behörde, Datum, Aktenzeichen) b) einliefernde Stelle	Einlieferung: Tag, Monat, Jahr, Stunde	Beendigung der Haft: Tag, Monat, Jahr, Stunde	Grund der Haftbeendigung	Nummer im Verzeichnis der abgenommenen Gegenstände	Abgelieferte Gelder und Wertsachen	Bestätigung der Richtigkeit aller Angaben u. der in Sp. 13 aufgeführten Gegenstände durch den Gefangenen	Hafttage	Bemerkungen
1	2	3	4	5	6	7	8	9	10	11	12	13	14	15	16

Nineteen-year-old Izabela Ucinska was sent to the Russian Glade “labour education camp” following an escape attempt.

“It was an atrocious camp […] There was no water, we didn’t wash. We were covered in mud, because during the gymnastics the ground became soft underfoot and we were up to the ankles in mud. I don’t know how I endured it.”

Memoirs of Izabela Ucinska in: Geraubte Leben: Zwangsarbeiter berichten, (Hg.): Stiftung EVZ, Köln/Weimar 2008, S. 35.

Ivan Kondratenko from Ukraine, just turned 18, was transported to the labour education camp.

“It was a death camp of sorts. They took me there. There was a long barracks, and gravel all around. After the interrogation, they made us run around the barracks: “Run, lie down, sit down! Run, lie down, sit down!” We ran barefoot on the gravel. Then they herded us into a corner and sprayed us down with a fire hose. When we went to bed, we had to climb four steps to the barracks, where we were counted with whiplashes. […] I was there for 14 days. Afterwards, I calculated that I got about 290 in those 14 days. I’m not sure, maybe more, some 300 lashes.”

Zwangsarbeit 1939–1945
Recollections of Iwan Kondratenko, Erinnerungen und Geschichte, Digitales Archiv für Bildung und Wissenschaft, TRANSKRIPT (Dt. Übersetzung): Kondratenko, Iwan Jakowitsch (Archiv-ID ZA485)

Camp Locations 1942/43

● Barracks for civilian forced labourers

Besides the POW camp, there were hundreds of barracks and camps for civilian forced labourers and soldiers in *work details* across the city. They lived in gym halls, inns, bombed out school buildings, barracks and company camps.

① Mixed camp, Regensburger Straße 215

From 1940, camp with barracks for prisoners of war and civilian forced labourers of different nationalities. They worked for municipal departments and private companies. In 1942, an additional area was set up for the arms manufacturer Diehl.

② "Russian glade"

A forest glade named after Russian prisoners of wars in the First World War. As of April 1942, a transit camp for *Eastern workers [Ostarbeiter],* and from summer 1942, an early camp for Soviet forced labourers.

③ "Russian glade"

Work education camp for civilian forced labourers from autumn 1942 to August 1943.

④ Former SS rally participants camp

As of 1943, barracks for around 1,000 civilian forced labourers from western and southern Europe who worked for MAN.

⑤ Prisoner of war camp

a. 1939 to 1945 stalag/oflag
b. August 1941 to around spring 1943 unofficial *Russian camp*

⑥ SS barracks

1941–45 a satellite camp of Dachau concentration camp, Flossenbürg concentration camp later took over responsibility for their administration. In Nuremberg, only a few concentration camp prisoners were used as forced labour, presumably due to the large number of prisoners of war and civilian forced labourers.

↗ Stadtarchiv Nürnberg, Dokumentationszentrum Reichsparteitagsgelände
Aerial photograph December 1944 NCAP (National Collection of Aerial Photography) US7/0035/A, 7040

1
2
3
4
5
6
a
b

“Work Details” in Nuremberg

Hard Work for the Wartime Economy

An industrial metropolis, Nuremberg’s demand for foreign workers was high. At the beginning of the war, prisoners of war and civilian forced labourers mainly worked on farms. As of 1942, they were deployed increasingly in the armaments industry – in the case of soldiers, in breach of international law.

Aside from arms manufacturers, the Nuremberg city council was one of the main employers from 1940 onwards. Ultimately, all sectors of Nuremberg society benefited from this. Many companies, commercial enterprises and trades, churches and even private households used forced labourers – as did also the Special-purpose Association Nazi Party Rallies [Zweckverband Reichsparteitagsgelände]. During the war, around 100,000 civilian forced labourers and thousands of prisoners of war maintained Nuremberg’s wartime economy.

Luigi Collo, Italian military internee, in his memoirs 1979

"... were deployed to clear the rubble in the city and put into paper bags the remains of thousands of people killed and blown to pieces by the bombing."

O ti arrangi o crepi. Un alpino nei lager tedeschi, settembre 1943-settembre 1945, Milano 1979

Perilous Work

As a major city and industrial hub, Nuremberg was ranked first priority as an air raid target. However, in most cases forced labourers and prisoners of war were denied access to shelters. After attacks, they had to risk their lives clearing rubble and removing bombs.

↑ Nuremberg around 1944
Stadtarchiv Nürnberg A57 L-060-34

Female Forced Labourers at Diehl

Some female workers at Diehl in Nuremberg removed the discriminatory *Eastern workers badge* for the photo. Wearing it became mandatory for Polish and Soviet civilians in 1940. The reason for taking the photo is not known.

← Female forced labourers of Metall-, Guß- & Preßwerk Heinrich Diehl, Nuremberg, 1942, photo: Antonina Batjuk, Lewowka (Ukraine), from the book „Die steinerne Rose" by Barbara Ostyn (Jablonska), Berlin 2003

Barbara Jablonska in an interview 2003

“I thought that the dispute over compensating [forced labourers] was a scandal […], because it revealed a cruel indifference, a cold wind from the past.”

↗ Barbara Jablonska 2003, interview Gerhard Jochem
↓ Barbara Jablonska after 1945, property of the Martineau family

Site of the Perpetrators

Barbara Jablonska (fourth on left), with former Nuremberg forced labourers and their families on the observation platform of the Documentation Center Former Nazi Party Rally Grounds, on the occasion of the first Nuremberg contemporary witness interview in 2002. Her book *Die steinerne Rose* was published a year later.

↑ Mrs Verbaan-Lisowska and her son Piotr (kneeling), the Kotlinskis, Ms Jablonska, Mrs Augusto, the Zweermans and Mr Augusto
Verlag testimon (Susanne Rieger)

Barbara Jablonska
1925–2015

Barbara Jablonska was born in a small town in southeast Galicia to Polish parents. Her mother came from a Jewish family. As a teenager, she witnessed the Soviet occupation and the invasion of the Wehrmacht two years later. In search of work, in May 1942 she was recruited as a *foreign worker* and taken to Nuremberg.

She remained until June 1943, living in different camps for female civilian forced workers, employed as an interpreter and as a worker in various companies. In summer 1943, armed with a leave certificate and counterfeit worker's ID card, she returned to Poland, where she lived until 1945 in constant fear of discovery and arrest. She emigrated to France in the 1970s.

Jerzy Zakrzewski in an interview 2015

"… there were only women and children. I dug them out willingly even though they were Germans. They were people, after all."

↗ Video collection Centralne Muzeum Jeńców Wojennych Nr. 108
↓ Jerzy Zakrzewski after the liberation 1945, private collection Marek Zakrzewski

Jerzy Zakrzewski
1928–2019

Jerzy Zakrzewski was born in Warsaw and joined the *Szare Szeregi [Grey Ranks]* scout movement in 1943. As part of the Polish Home Army, a military resistance organisation, the scouts fought to free Poland in the Warsaw Uprising. He survived the fighting and after the Home Army capitulated in October 1944 he was captured by the Germans.

Like many others from the Warsaw Uprising, Zakrzewski ended up in the Langwasser prisoner of war camp. He had to recover people and corpses buried under the rubble. After the war, he initially remained in Germany, completing his Abitur qualification before returning to Poland in 1947. He became an engineer and started a family.

Langwasser Camp
After the liberation in April 1945, the former prisoner of war camp became an important assembly centre for the repatriation of Polish prisoners of war and forced labourers.

← Jerzy Zakrzewski (extreme left) 1945
Centralne Muzeum Jeńców Wojennych,
Materiały i Dokumenty Nr. 6380

Commonplace Exclusion

The Nazi state's *foreign labour* policy was an object of conflicting tensions arising from economic necessity and Nazi racial ideology. Numerous regulations were designed to control the conduct of Germans towards prisoners of war and civilian forced labourers and to ensconce a social order based on racial hierarchy: forced labourers and soldiers from the Soviet Union, Poland and, from 1943 onwards, Italy, held far fewer rights than West Europeans.

In their role as employers, foremen, guards and informers, many Germans excluded male and female deportees from society. They also harassed and exposed them to security police sanctions, some of which resulted in death. Foreign forced labourers were a common sight for Nuremberg's citizens. Any contact was strictly forbidden.

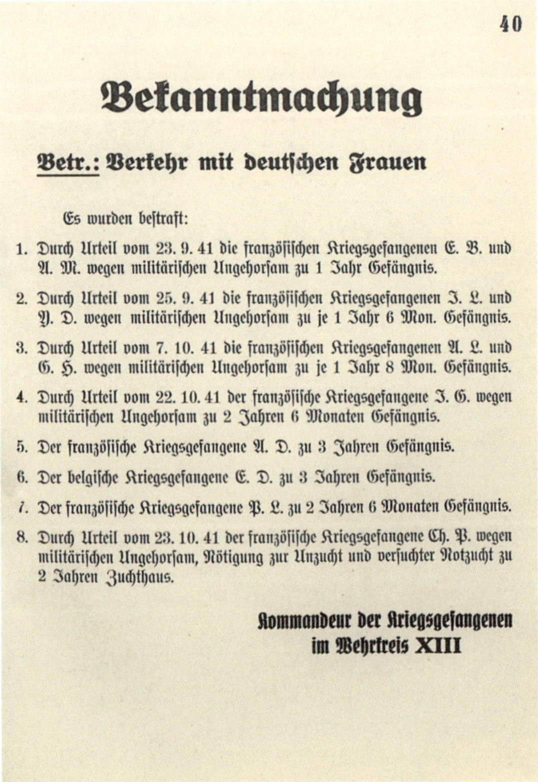

40

Bekanntmachung

Betr.: Verkehr mit deutschen Frauen

Es wurden bestraft:

1. Durch Urteil vom 23. 9. 41 die französischen Kriegsgefangenen E. B. und A. M. wegen militärischen Ungehorsam zu 1 Jahr Gefängnis.
2. Durch Urteil vom 25. 9. 41 die französischen Kriegsgefangenen J. L. und Y. D. wegen militärischen Ungehorsam zu je 1 Jahr 6 Mon. Gefängnis.
3. Durch Urteil vom 7. 10. 41 die französischen Kriegsgefangenen A. L. und G. H. wegen militärischen Ungehorsam zu je 1 Jahr 8 Mon. Gefängnis.
4. Durch Urteil vom 22. 10. 41 der französische Kriegsgefangene J. G. wegen militärischen Ungehorsam zu 2 Jahren 6 Monaten Gefängnis.
5. Der französische Kriegsgefangene A. D. zu 3 Jahren Gefängnis.
6. Der belgische Kriegsgefangene E. D. zu 3 Jahren Gefängnis.
7. Der französische Kriegsgefangene P. L. zu 2 Jahren 6 Monaten Gefängnis.
8. Durch Urteil vom 23. 10. 41 der französische Kriegsgefangene Ch. P. wegen militärischen Ungehorsam, Nötigung zur Unzucht und versuchter Notzucht zu 2 Jahren Zuchthaus.

Kommandeur der Kriegsgefangenen im Wehrkreis XIII

Severe Sanctions

Military courts actively pursued any breaches of relationship and contact regulations, the consequences of which were effectively and widely publicised. In contrast to soldiers from the West, any relationships with German women usually carried the death penalty for soldiers from Poland and the Soviet Union.

↑ Announcement 1941
Bundesarchiv RH 38/170, Bl. 39/40

Gift or "Bread Currency"

Not all Germans abused their power. Despite the bans, contacts were numerous and in hindsight, difficult to interpret. Items made by forced labourers, like this wooden toy, were a token of gratitude for acts of human sympathy or served as bread currency [Brotwährung] in barter transactions.
This example from the Würzburg area:
`one parrot + one small plane`
`= three pounds of bread`

→ Wooden parrot 1940/45
Fränkisches Freilandmuseum Bad Windsheim Nr. 15/234/
exhibit photography: Tim Hufnagel

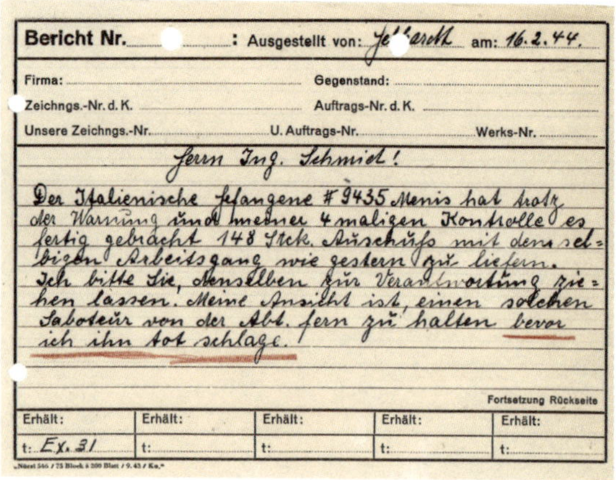

Bericht Nr. .... : Ausgestellt von: [illegible] am: 16.2.44.

Firma: .... Gegenstand: ....
Zeichngs.-Nr. d. K. .... Auftrags-Nr. d. K. ....
Unsere Zeichngs.-Nr. .... U. Auftrags-Nr. .... Werks-Nr. ....

Herrn Ing. Schmidt!
Der Italienische Gefangene #9435 Menis hat trotz der Warnung und meiner 4maligen Kontrolle es fertig gebracht 148 Stck. Ausschuß mit denselbigen Arbeitsgang wie gestern zu liefern. Ich bitte Sie, denselben zur Verantwortung ziehen lassen. Meine Ansicht ist, einen solchen Saboteur von der Abt. fern zu halten bevor ich ihn tot schlage.

Fortsetzung Rückseite

Erhält:	Erhält:	Erhält:	Erhält:	Erhält:
t: Ex. 31	t:	t:	t:	t:

Abuse of Power

Many German guards and employers took advantage of the powers conferred on them. They withheld wages, cut food rations and subjected their victims to verbal or physical abuse. Penalties were harshest for those accused of sabotage.

↑ Report 1944
The U.S. National Archives and Records Administration Identifier 581103, box 384, file 66-24

Fritz Munkert during interrogation by the Gestapo on 8 October 1943

“It is true to say that I still do not share the National Socialist world view, because I cannot reconcile myself to this new mentality.”

↗ Bundesarchiv R3017/34086
↓ Fritz Munkert 1940s, private property

Spione Verräter Saboteure!

Wer von unseren Gefolgschaftsmitgliedern die Tageszeitungen aufmerksam liest, findet immer wieder Gerichtsurteile wegen unerlaubte Beziehungen mit Ausländern oder Lieferung von Unterlagen an den feindlichen Nachrichtendienst. Erst kürzlich wurden wieder zwei Volksdeutsche hingerichtet, welche nur aus Gewinnsucht im Auftrag eines fremden Nachrichtendienstes deutsche Befestigungsanlagen ausgekundschaftet oder Reisen in Deutschland unternommen haben, um deutsche Staatsgeheimnisse auszuspähen.

Tod oder langjährige Zuchthausstrafen sind stets die Folgen eines solchen verwerflichen Tuns. Gerade in der Zeit, in welcher das gesamte deutsche Volk in erbittertem zähem Abwehrkampf seinen Feinden und damit dem gesamten Judentum der Welt gegenübersteht, kann eine solche Handlungsweise gar nicht scharf genug geahndet werden.

Immer wieder werden vor deutschen Sondergerichten Rundfunkverbrecher abgeurteilt, die sich durch Abhören ausländischer Rundfunksender und Weitergabe der von ihnen verbreiteten Nachrichten zu Verrätern an ihrem Volk und seinem Daseinskampf gemacht hatten.

In letzter Zeit häufen sich die Fälle, in welchen schwere Zuchthausstrafen über würdelose Frauen und Männer ausgesprochen wurden, welche verbotenen Umgang mit Kriegsgefangenen gepflogen haben, sei es, daß sie mit Kriegsgefangenen in Briefwechsel traten, ihnen Rauch- und Eßwaren, Getränke usw. zusteckten oder andere verbotene Beziehungen mit ihnen unterhielten und damit bar jeder Scham auf die schwerste Weise die nationale Würde des deutschen Volkes verletzt haben.

Es wird bei dieser Gelegenheit auf die kürzlich an den schwarzen Brettern unserer Werke angeschlagene Bekanntmachung über den verbotenen Umgang mit Kriegsgefangenen vom 19. Februar 1941 verwiesen. Von unserer Gefolgschaft wird daher in ihrem eigenen Interesse erwartet, daß sie nach dem Grundsatz

„Feind bleibt Feind!“

Kriegsgefangene sowohl innerhalb als auch außerhalb des Werkes entsprechend behandelt.

13

“An enemy is always an enemy!”
Siemens never tired of regularly reminding its German workforce that any contact with forced labourers was strictly prohibited. The notice was printed in the company newspaper *Das Nürnberger Werk.*

↑ Notice *An enemy is always an enemy!*
in: Das Nürnberger Werk/Siemens Betriebszeitung, Nürnberg 1941

Fritz Munkert
1888–1944

Fritz Munkert was born in Nuremberg, worked for Siemens and was a staunch Social Democrat. In 1935, he was arrested for his involvement in the social democratic resistance movement and imprisoned in Dachau for two and a half years until 1939.

On his release, he returned to his job at Siemens. An act of humanity and criticism of the regime proved fateful for him. His colleague, SA leader Georg Schönegger witnessed Fritz Munkert making critical remarks about the course of the war and another colleague saw him giving cigarettes to a Soviet forced labourer. In 1943, he was denounced by Schönegger. Fritz Munkert was accused of allegedly *subverting the war* effort and sentenced to death. He was executed in 1944.

↓ Teodor Kazarowicz 1940s, Dokumentationszentrum Reichsparteitagsgelände Ph-1307-01

Teodor Kazarowicz
1915–1962

Teodor Kazarowicz was born in 1915, close to the present-day border between Belarus and Lithuania. In the wake of the war between Poland and the Soviet Union his homeland fell to Poland in the 1920s. Called up at the beginning of the Second World War in 1939, he was taken prisoner and interned in Langwasser.

In June 1940, he was detailed to work for a farmer in rural Buch, near Nuremberg – initially as a prisoner of war, later as a civilian forced labourer. At the farm, he met and fell in love with the farmer's daughter Kunigunde Hofmann. Discovery would have meant the death penalty for him and a concentration camp for her. However, the relationship between Teodor Kazarowicz and Kunigunde Hofmann remained a secret from the authorities.

Wedding
The couple married in 1945. They stayed in Nuremberg and had two daughters.

↑ Wedding photo 1945
Dokumentationszentrum Reichsparteitagsgelände Ph-1307-02

A Place of Brutality

Mass Deaths in the "Russian Camp"

The attack on the Soviet Union in June 1941 heralded a ramping up of the war of extermination in Eastern Europe. The death of millions of civilians and prisoners of war in the Soviet Union was calculated. In its treatment of Soviet prisoners the Nazi regime deliberately flouted international conventions. At the beginning of August 1941, Soviet prisoners of war arrived at March Field station. More were to follow.

Barely alive, they were interned at the unofficial *Russian camp* within view of the officers' camp. The conditions at the camp were catastrophic. Regardless of their physical condition, thousands were sent on *work details.* By the time it was disbanded in 1943, hundreds of soldiers had died in the unofficial *Russian camp* in Langwasser.

Suffering in the "Russian Camp"
In winter 1941, hundreds of men died of malnutrition, cold and a lack of medical care. Guard Karl Bach documented the prisoners' situation in photos. In spring 1942, he photographed a group of prisoners in front of their tent.

↑ Soviet prisoners of war 1942
Dokumentationszentrum Reichsparteitagsgelände Ph-0401-06

Death on the March Field
1,400 sowjet soldiers remained at the camp. From October 1941 they were assigned to the Special-purpose Association Nazi Party Rallies as *work detail* 298. Engaged in gruelling excavation work on the March Field, within a short time more than 935 died of exhaustion and at the hands of the guards.

↑ Guards on March Field 1941
Dokumentationszentrum Reichsparteitagsgelände Ph-0401-18

Otto Madl in a letter 1941

"And how hungry they are. They gobble up every bug and worm they see on the ground."

↗ Property of the Blumtritt family/Museum für Kommunikation Berlin
↓ Otto Madl 1940s, property of the Blumtritt family/Museum für Kommunikation, Berlin

Otto Madl
1907–1945

Otto Madl was born in Neukirchen, Bavaria. A printer by trade, he worked as a farmer. In 1940 he was drafted by the Wehrmacht and deployed as a guard in the officers' camp in Langwasser. In countless letters to his family, he railed against his guard duties and openly described the disastrous living conditions of the Soviet prisoners of war.

In 1941, with revulsion and horror, he reported cannibalism in the Langwasser *Russian camp*. Otto Madl was later dispatched to the Eastern Front and died in Soviet captivity in February 1945.

Utter Despair
The photo of Soviet prisoners of war, desperately searching for food, was unemotionally captioned by Otto Madl in his album as *Russians eating grass*.

↑ Otto Madl's photo album 1941
Property of the Blumtritt family/Museum für Kommunikation, Berlin

Deliberate Murder of Soviet Prisoners of War

Along with the Soviet prisoners of war, the Nazi regime brought its brutal and ideological war to the German Reich. Mainly Soviet soldiers died as a result of inhuman conditions in camps on German soil set up specifically for them. At the same time, in July 1941 the Wehrmacht, Gestapo and SS began to systematically murder more than 30,000 Soviet prisoners. These so-called *selections [Aussonderungen]* were one of the major crimes committed on German soil.

Aided by the camp commandants, Gestapo task forces inspected the Soviet prisoners. The criteria applied in their search for *political commissars, intellectuals* and *Jews* – so-called *intolerable elements* – were frequently arbitrary. More than 2,300 Soviet soldiers from the Langwasser *Russian camp* and the military district were selected and sent to Dachau for execution. Only the increased use of forced labour as of 1942 halted the killing.

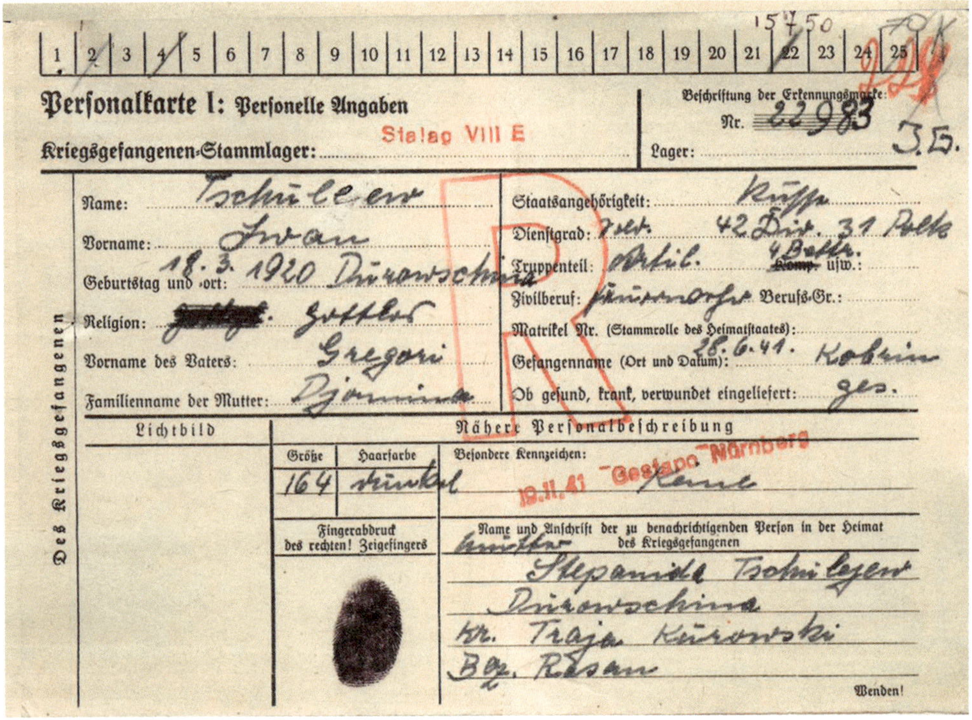

1 2 3 4 5 6 7 8 9 10 11 12 13 14 15 16 17 18 19 20 21 22 23 24 25

Personalkarte I: Personelle Angaben

Kriegsgefangenen-Stammlager: Stalag VIII E

Beschriftung der Erkennungsmarke: Nr. 22983 Lager:

Name: Tschuleew

Vorname: Iwan

Geburtstag und -ort: 18.3.1920 Dürowschina

Religion: gottlos

Vorname des Vaters: Gregori

Familienname der Mutter: Djomina

Staatsangehörigkeit: Russe

Dienstgrad: Sold. 42 Div. 31 Regt.

Truppenteil: Artil. 4 Battr. Komp. usw.:

Zivilberuf: Berufs-Gr.:

Matrikel Nr. (Stammrolle des Heimatstaates):

Gefangennahme (Ort und Datum): 28.6.41. Kobrin

Ob gesund, krank, verwundet eingeliefert: ges.

Des Kriegsgefangenen

Lichtbild

Nähere Personalbeschreibung

Größe: 164 Haarfarbe: dunkel

Besondere Kennzeichen: Keine

19.11.41 Gestapo Nürnberg

Fingerabdruck des rechten! Zeigefingers

Name und Anschrift der zu benachrichtigenden Person in der Heimat des Kriegsgefangenen: Mutter Stepanida Tschuleew Dürowschina Kr. Traja Kurowski Bez. Rasan

Wenden!

Deregistration, then Dachau

The responsible Wehrmacht department bureaucratically noted its involvement in the murder on the prisoners' files. With its stamp *Gestapo Nürnberg*, the Wehrmacht deregistered Iwan Tschuleew from its area of responsibility, in full awareness of his future fate.

↑ Personal file 1941
obd. memorial No. 915518282

Wladimir Poltawskij on the back of the photo to his son in 1941

"My son, kiss me here on the photo and I kiss you."

↗ Property of Alexandr Poltawskij
↓ Wladimir Poltawskij 1941, property of Alexandr Poltawskij

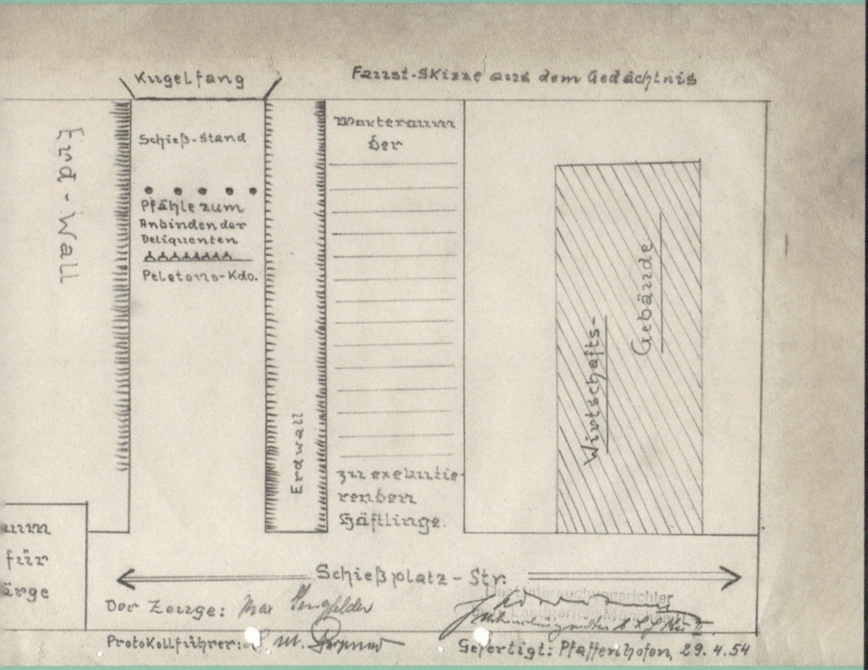

Wladimir Poltawskij
1919–1941

Wladimir Poltawskij was born in a small village in the southern Russian region of Rostov-on-Don. After the early death of his parents, he was brought up in a children's home. He worked as a clerk on archaeological excavations. Married in 1940, to his great regret he was drafted in 1941.

Just a few days after the Wehrmacht attack, he was taken prisoner and sent to the unofficial *Langwasser Russian camp.* He survived *work detail* 298 on the March Field, but in November 1941 was *selected* by the Nuremberg-Fürth Gestapo task force and, aged just 22, was shot on the SS shooting range in Hebertshausen near Dachau.

Hebertshausen Shooting Range

"My mother could hear the shooting for days on end, because we lived near the shooting range. The shooting went on every day for weeks and lasted into the evening."

Maria Seidenberger in an interview 2001
Property of Christoph Riedelsheimer
↑ Sketch of the Hebertshausen shooting range from investigation proceedings 1954
Staatsarchiv München Staatsanwaltschaften 34871/6 (fol. 231)

Deportation of Jews from Northern Bavaria

The swift victory in the Russian campaign did not materialise and the Nazi leaders decided not to postpone the systematic murder of European Jews any longer. In October 1941, the deportation of Jewish Germans to ghettos and extermination camps began. The forced departure from their home towns was witnessed by the population.

An assembly point on the edge of the rally grounds was the last stage before their deportation for more than 2,000 Jews from northern Bavaria. Once there, they were harassed, mistreated and robbed of their property. In November 1941, a deportation took place from March Field station to the improvised Jungfernhof camp near Riga, and in March 1942, another to Izbica ghetto in Poland. Only 52 of those deported to Riga survived the Holocaust. No-one returned from Izbica.

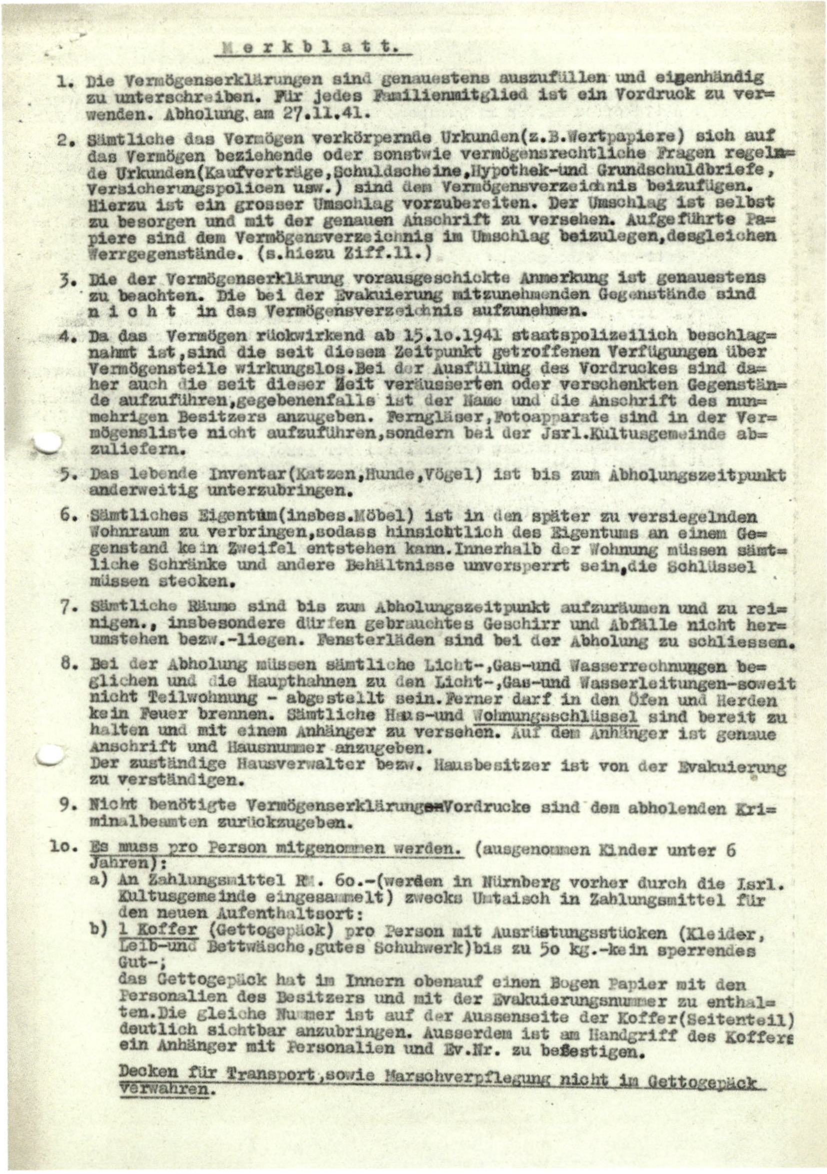

Merkblatt.

1. Die Vermögenserklärungen sind genauestens auszufüllen und eigenhändig zu unterschreiben. Für jedes Familienmitglied ist ein Vordruck zu ver=wenden. Abholung am 27.11.41.

2. Sämtliche das Vermögen verkörpernde Urkunden(z.B.Wertpapiere) sich auf das Vermögen beziehende oder sonstwie vermögensrechtliche Fragen regeln=de Urkunden(Kaufverträge,Schuldscheine,Hypothek-und Grundschuldbriefe, Versicherungspolicen usw.) sind dem Vermögensverzeichnis beizufügen. Hierzu ist ein grosser Umschlag vorzubereiten. Der Umschlag ist selbst zu besorgen und mit der genauen Anschrift zu versehen. Aufgeführte Pa=piere sind dem Vermögensverzeichnis im Umschlag beizulegen,desgleichen Werrgegenstände. (s.hiezu Ziff.11.)

3. Die der Vermögenserklärung vorausgeschickte Anmerkung ist genauestens zu beachten. Die bei der Evakuierung mitzunehmenden Gegenstände sind n i c h t in das Vermögensverzeichnis aufzunehmen.

4. Da das Vermögen rückwirkend ab 15.10.1941 staatspolizeilich beschlag=nahmt ist,sind die seit diesem Zeitpunkt getroffenen Verfügungen über Vermögensteile wirkungslos.Bei der Ausfüllung des Vordruckes sind da=her auch die seit dieser Zeit veräusserten oder verschenkten Gegenstän=de aufzuführen,gegebenenfalls ist der Name und die Anschrift des nun=mehrigen Besitzers anzugeben. Ferngläser,Fotoapparate sind in der Ver=mögensliste nicht aufzuführen,sondern bei der Jsrl.Kultusgemeinde ab=zuliefern.

5. Das lebende Inventar(Katzen,Hunde,Vögel) ist bis zum Abholungszeitpunkt anderweitig unterzubringen.

6. Sämtliches Eigentum(insbes.Möbel) ist in den später zu versiegelnden Wohnraum zu verbringen,sodass hinsichtlich des Eigentums an einem Ge=genstand kein Zweifel entstehen kann.Innerhalb der Wohnung müssen sämt=liche Schränke und andere Behältnisse unversperrt sein,die Schlüssel müssen stecken.

7. Sämtliche Räume sind bis zum Abholungszeitpunkt aufzuräumen und zu rei=nigen., insbesondere dürfen gebrauchtes Geschirr und Abfälle nicht her=umstehen bezw.-liegen. Fensterläden sind bei der Abholung zu schliessen.

8. Bei der Abholung müssen sämtliche Licht-,Gas-und Wasserrechnungen be=glichen und die Haupthahnen zu den Licht-,Gas-und Wasserleitungen-soweit nicht Teilwohnung - abgestellt sein.Ferner darf in den Öfen und Herden kein Feuer brennen. Sämtliche Haus-und Wohnungsschlüssel sind bereit zu halten und mit einem Anhänger zu versehen. Auf dem Anhänger ist genaue Anschrift und Hausnummer anzugeben.
Der zuständige Hausverwalter bezw. Hausbesitzer ist von der Evakuierung zu verständigen.

9. Nicht benötigte VermögenserklärungenVordrucke sind dem abholenden Kri=minalbeamten zurückzugeben.

10. Es muss pro Person mitgenommen werden. (ausgenommen Kinder unter 6 Jahren):
a) An Zahlungsmittel RM. 60.-(werden in Nürnberg vorher durch die Isrl. Kultusgemeinde eingesammelt) zwecks Umtaisch in Zahlungsmittel für den neuen Aufenthaltsort:
b) 1 Koffer (Gettogepäck) pro Person mit Ausrüstungsstücken (Kleider, Leib-und Bettwäsche,gutes Schuhwerk)bis zu 50 kg.-kein sperrendes Gut-;
das Gettogepäck hat im Innern obenauf einen Bogen Papier mit den Personalien des Besitzers und mit der Evakuierungsnummer zu enthal=ten.Die gleiche Nummer ist auf der Aussenseite der Koffer(Seitenteil) deutlich sichtbar anzubringen. Ausserdem ist am Handgriff des Koffers ein Anhänger mit Personalien und Ev.Nr. zu befestigen.
Decken für Transport,sowie Marschverpflegung nicht im Gettogepäck verwahren.

Orderly Deportation

Within a few days, people were brutally wrenched from their homes. There was scarcely any time to satisfy the detailed provisions prior to deportation. They had to leave with just a few possessions.

← Police bulletin 1941
Zentralarchiv zur Erforschung der Geschichte der Juden in Deutschland
Bestand B.1/19 (Israelitische Religionsgemeinschaft Baden) Nr. 333

Pictures of Deportation

The Nuremberg-Fürth Gestapo documented the deportation of Jews from Nuremberg in photos and film. The film, which has not survived, was shown at a *social evening [Kameradschaftsabend]* for the entertainment of the officers.

↑ Nuremberg Jews on the way to the assembly camp 1941
Private property

Siegfried Reinhold, a Nuremberg Jew,
in his 1945 report on the journey to the Jungfernhof camp near Riga

"We grieved for the first dead and missing in the evening; they had probably been unable to keep up on the very icy roads and were shot."

Wiener Holocaust Library 1656/3/8/285

Inscription on the photo shortly before deportation in 1942

“Dear Dolfi, a little memento from your faithful friend Miri.”

↗ Stadtarchiv Nürnberg F 14 Nr. 4
↓ Miriam Blumenthal around 1940, Stadtarchiv Nürnberg F 14 Nr. 4

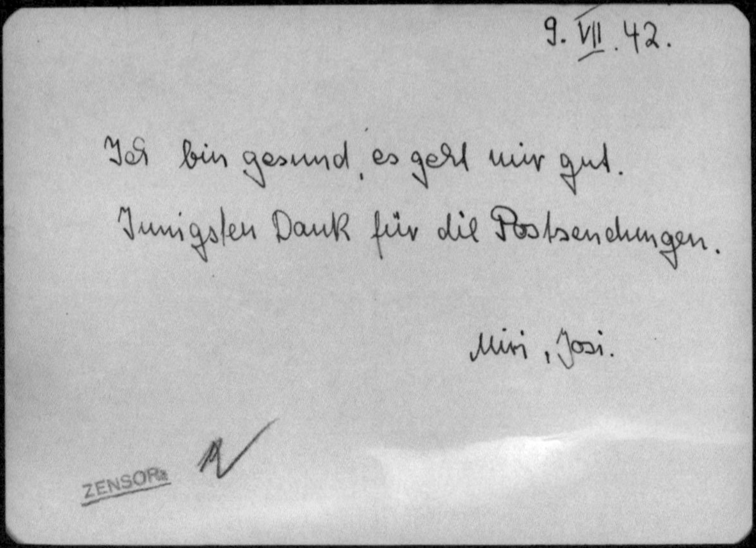

9. VII. 42.

Ich bin gesund, es geht mir gut.
Innigsten Dank für die Postsendungen.

Miri, Josi.

ZENSOR

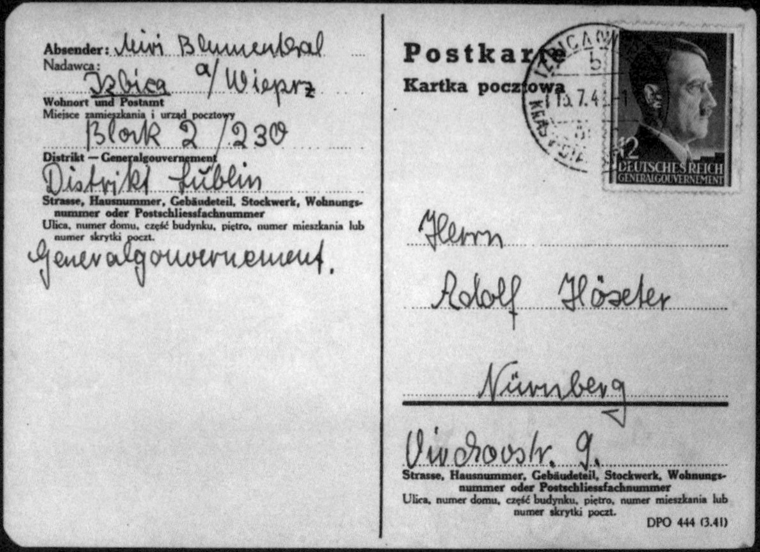

Absender: Miri Blumenthal
Nadawca:
Izbica a/Wieprz
Wohnort und Postamt
Miejsce zamieszkania i urząd pocztowy
Block 2/230
Distrikt — Generalgouvernement
Distrikt Lublin
Strasse, Hausnummer, Gebäudeteil, Stockwerk, Wohnungsnummer oder Postschliessfachnummer
Ulica, numer domu, część budynku, piętro, numer mieszkania lub numer skrytki poczt.
Generalgouvernement.

Postkarte
Kartka pocztowa

42 DEUTSCHES REICH GENERALGOUVERNEMENT

Herrn
Adolf Höseler
Nürnberg
Virchowstr. 9.
Strasse, Hausnummer, Gebäudeteil, Stockwerk, Wohnungsnummer oder Postschliessfachnummer
Ulica, numer domu, część budynku, piętro, numer mieszkania lub numer skrytki poczt.
DPO 444 (3.41)

Miriam Blumenthal 1926–1942

Miriam Blumenthal lived with her sister Josepha and mother Gisela in Bärenschanzstraße, Nuremberg. All three women were deported on 24 March 1942 from March Field station to the Izbica ghetto in Poland. There, all trace is lost.

Last Contact

After the censored postcard from Izbica dated July 1942, from Miriam Blumenthal to her friend in Nuremberg, contact ceased.

← Postcard 1942
Stadtarchiv Nürnberg F 14 Nr. 4

Rock in Park

Most of the year Dutzendteich park is a recreational area for Nuremberg's inhabitants. Various major events in the summer attract tens of thousands of visitors, the historical buildings often only forming a backdrop.

↓ Rock in Park 2013
Stadt Nürnberg/Uwe Niklas

1945
-2020

1945 2020

No Ordinary Place – Approaching the Rally Grounds

Nuremberg in April 1945: the US Army celebrated its victory over National Socialist Nuremberg with a parade on Zeppelin Field. In November, the Allies held the leading Nazis accountable in the *Nuremberg Trial of the Major War Criminals.*

While the old town lay in ruins, the rally grounds survived the war more or less unscathed. Many other cities in the Federal Republic of Germany simply continued to use buildings dating from the Nazi period. In Nuremberg, the sheer size of the buildings precluded swift repurposing. For decades, the urban community has sought an approach to the rally grounds.

The generational change in the 1960s sparked a rethink in Germany with regard to Nazism. The *Nuremberg Discussions [Nürnberger Gespräche]* were an early attempt to address the Nazi past. In the mid-1980s the first information services and tours of the rally grounds as a historic site were offered. The Documentation Center, opened in 2001, became a magnet for tourists. However, problems also arose with the increasing use of the grounds. In the future, a meaningful balance should be sought between history, culture, leisure and economic interests.

Demolition of the March Field Towers

The March Field site remained largely unused after 1945. The towers were blown up in the middle of the 1960s and the Nuremberg Langwasser housing estate was built.

← Demolition of the March Field towers 1966
Archiv Bayerischer Rundfunk/Hans Kastner

Diverse Further Use

Immediately after the War

The years after 1945 were dominated by occupation policy and refugee flows. Conscious of its symbolic power, the US Army blew up the swastika on the Zeppelin Grandstand on April 22, 1945.

The internationally recognised trial of the main Nazi war criminals took place in Nuremberg. It was the first time that leading representatives of a state were held personally accountable for war crimes before an international military tribunal.

Initially, the Americans interned German prisoners in the former POW camp. Later, the barracks were used to house displaced persons, including former forced labourers and concentration camp prisoners, refugees and displaced persons from Eastern Europe. The last stone barracks in Langwasser were only demolished in 1965. A modern district was built in their place, providing housing for many Nuremberg citizens.

Americans in Nuremberg
US Army soldiers were stationed in Nuremberg from 1945 to 1994. Zeppelin Field, now renamed *Soldier's Field,* was used not only for military parades and shows, but also for sports events and German-American fun fairs.

← Zeppelin Grandstand in 1947
Dokumentationszentrum Reichsparteitagsgelände D-0305-01/Ray d'Addario

Nuremberg Trial

The Americans succeeded in having the *Trial of the Major War Criminals* held in their occupation zone. The intact court buildings and adjacent prison tipped the scale in Nuremberg's favour. Germans showed little interest in the trial, although by and large the sentences were welcomed.

↑ Nuremberg Trial 1945
Stadtarchiv Nürnberg A65_I-RD_137_D

Refugee Camp

Until 1964, displaced persons and refugees were housed in the former POW camp. At times, more than 4,000 people from many different countries lived in the primitive barracks of the transit camp.

↑ Federal holding camp for foreigners at the end of the 1950s
Geschichte Für Alle e.V.

Lazlo P. inmate of the refugee camp from 1951 to 1961, in an interview 1995

"… considering that several thousand people from more than 20 different nations lived together in such cramped conditions and coped with social tensions, it worked amazingly well."

Bernd Windsheimer: Langwasser. Geschichte eines Stadtteils, Nürnberg 2007.

Natascha Wodin in an interview 2018

“That was the feeling the outside world gave me. As a child that’s how I actually felt, like a piece of rubbish.”

↗ Susanne Führer: Schreiben ist eine Möglichkeit, Leben zu ersetzen. Deutschlandfunkkultur 21.8.2018
↓ Natascha Wodin around 2017, Rowohlt Verlag

Natascha Wodin
*1945

As the child of former Ukrainian forced labourers, Natascha Wodin spent part of her childhood in the Valka camp in Langwasser. Her mother died early and she became homeless after running away from her violent father. She graduated from language school, worked as an interpreter in Moscow and translated Russian literature.

In 1980, she began to write herself. Her stories are partly autobiographical and deal with uprootedness, searching for identity, and foreignness. In her novel *She came from Mariupol* Natascha Wodin describes the fate of her mother, who was a forced labourer in Germany. In 2017, she won an award for the work at the Leipzig Book Fair.

Early Loss

Natascha was eleven when her mother committed suicide. Her father sent her and her younger sister to a Catholic children’s home.

← The Wodins at the mother’s grave around 1956
Private archive Natascha Wodin

Political and Religious Appropriations

After the war, the rally grounds were deliberately chosen as a venue for events that demonstrated a clear political stance. The May Day celebration and a trade union gathering were a demonstrative statement against Nazism. By contrast, in their speeches, message and staging, the Sudeten German Days intentionally harked back to the Nazi Party Rallies.

Different religious groups used the Zeppelin Field. By holding services there, they aimed to present the grounds in a more positive light. Today, the historical site is no longer available for these partly dubious religious messages.

Trade Union Gathering

Trade unionists from Germany, Austria and France assembled in front of the Congress Hall in 1962. The motto *Their buildings are dead – conquer their spirit [Ihre Bauten sind tot – überwindet ihren Geist]* referred directly to the site's history and called for a new mindset and approach.

↑ Trade union gathering 1962
Picture-Alliance/dpa/Karl Schnoerrer

Sudeten German Day

On the coloured photograph of the Zeppelin Grandstand for Sudeten German Day, the *Soldier's Field* banner is covered over and the masses face the grandstand. The central section and podium are draped with coats of arms, badges and flags. The parallels to the Nazi era were not regarded as troublesome.

↑ Sudeten German Day on the Zeppelin Grandstand 1955
Dokumentationszentrum Reichsparteitagsgelände D-0307-01

World Congress

At the 1955 World Congress of Jehovah's Witnesses, the fist and crown of Jehovah, along with a canopy over the podium, replaced the Nazi symbols on the Zeppelin Grandstand. Around 100,000 people celebrated their faith under the motto of *Triumphant Kingdom [Triumphierendes Königreich]*.

↑ Postcard 1955
Dokumentationszentrum Reichsparteitagsgelände D-0308-01

Mass Evangelisation

In 1963, crowds flocked to Zeppelin Field for the mass evangelisation by Baptist preacher Billy Graham. Graham saw his events as crusades against unbelief and intentionally chose the podium of the Zeppelin Grandstand to proclaim his message.

→ Photo album 1963
Property of Andreas Hellmuth

Am 16. Juni 1963
auf der Zeppelinwiese
Billy Graham
bringt das Wort
Gottes
dem Menschen
unserer Zeit
12.–16. Juni

Pragmatic Use

The vast majority of Germany's postwar society tried to avoid a painful confrontation with the past. Given the massive war damage in Nuremberg, the Congress Hall was largely used as a main storage facility. This pragmatic approach is still upheld today.

The removal of Luitpold Arena in the 1950s and the March Field towers in the 1960s created space for new urban building projects – the Meistersingerhalle concert hall and Langwasser housing estate. Inconvenient history was disposed of conveniently. Only the blowing-up of the Zeppelin Grandstand colonnades in 1967 caused a controversy. Today, sports, music and leisure events dominate the scene at the restored Dutzendteich park.

Bob Dylan Concert

In 1978, at his legendary concert on Zeppelin Field, Bob Dylan sang *Masters of War* in an explicit condemnation of warmongers. The jubilant crowds invaded the grandstand. The concert definitively opened up the site for large-scale music events.

↑ Zeppelin Grandstand at the Dylan concert 1978
Property of Johann Gerdenitsch

Martin Droschke in his poem
"Rally grounds recreation area" 1995

"Amid in the fried bratwurst aroma from the portable grill, the flag salutes: Do you want the total experience. [...] Against the panorama of the Führer grand-stand, a swan on Dutzendteich lake, Hannes, with the Audi Club flag fluttering above, turns and adds more sausages."

Laufschrift. Magazin für Literatur und Kunst 1/1995

Pedalo Legend

Until its destruction by the Nazis, Dutzendteich lake and its natural environs, restaurants and boats was a popular attraction for Nuremberg's citizens. Today, the swan-shaped pedalo is a symbol of the restored recreational area in the southeast of the city.

↑ Swan-shaped pedalo on Dutzendteich Lake 2015
Dokumentationszentrum Reichsparteitagsgelände D-0309-01/Helmut Meyer zur Capellen/photomontage: Kommunikationsdesign Martin Küchle

Norisring Race

The first race around Zeppelin Grandstand was held in 1947. This conscious decision by the city council was aimed at superimposing a popular leisure experience on the Nazi past. Today, the race is increasingly controversial.

↑ Norisring Car Race 2008
Stadt Nürnberg/Ralf Schedlbauer

Classic Open Air
Since 2000, more than 160,000 people have attended the concerts every year, picknicking peacefully together on the former parade ground of the SS and SA.

↑ Concert in Luitpold Grove 2013
Stadt Nürnberg/Uwe Niklas

Quelle Warehouse, Congress Hall
The planned demolition and conversion of the Congress Hall foundered due to the costs. In order to use the existing space profitably, in 1972 the city rented a large part of the Congress Hall to the mail order company Quelle. Until its bankruptcy in 2006, Quelle dispatched merchandise from Nuremberg to all over the country.

↑ *Quelle Suppliers!* sign around 1980
Dokumentationszentrum Reichsparteitagsgelände DZO-0143-0/
exhibit photography: Tim Hufnagl

Controversial Demolition

In 1967, due to their state of disrepair, the Zeppelin Grandstand colonnades were blown up by order of the mayor. This destruction of part of the building was hotly debated. In public the impression arose that the state of the building had provided a welcome opportunity to quickly remove unwanted relics of the Nazi era.

↑ Rubble from the colonnades 1967
Dokumentationszentrum Reichsparteitagsgelände DZO-014/
exhibit photography: Stefan Meyer

Changed Perception

Critical Awareness

In the 1960s, many Germans continued to block out the Nazi past. Nuremberg's cultural officer Hermann Glaser launched the city's engagement with Nazi history in a series of discussions. On his initiative, in 1984 a multi-media show on the subject, unique in Germany, was mounted in the Zeppelin Grandstand.

In 2001, in the north wing of the Congress Hall, a listed building since 1973, the Documentation Center Nazi Party Rally Grounds was opened. The permanent exhibition explains the history of the rallies and the grounds. The design by Günther Domenig was adamant in its rejection of monumental architecture.

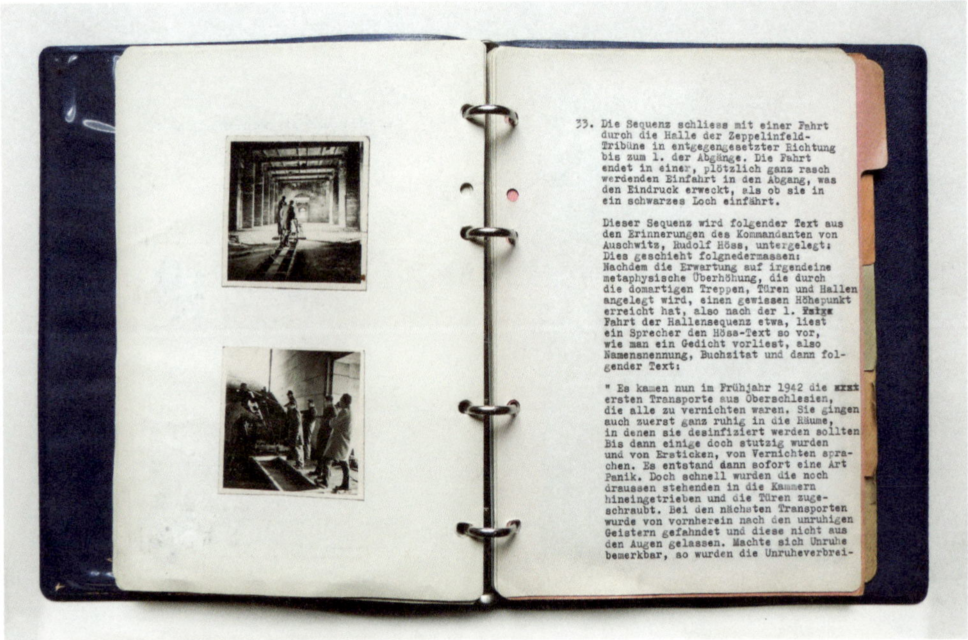

33. Die Sequenz schliess mit einer Fahrt durch die Halle der Zeppelinfeld-Tribüne in entgegengesetzter Richtung bis zum 1. der Abgänge. Die Fahrt endet in einer, plötzlich ganz rasch werdenden Einfahrt in den Abgang, was den Eindruck erweckt, als ob sie in ein schwarzes Loch einfährt.

Dieser Sequenz wird folgender Text aus den Erinnerungen des Kommandanten von Auschwitz, Rudolf Höss, untergelegt: Dies geschieht folgnedermassen: Nachdem die Erwartung auf irgendeine metaphysische Überhöhung, die durch die domartigen Treppen, Türen und Hallen angelegt wird, einen gewissen Höhepunkt erreicht hat, also nach der 1. Fahrt der Hallensequenz etwa, liest ein Sprecher den Höss-Text so vor, wie man ein Gedicht vorliest, also Namensnennung, Buchzitat und dann folgender Text:

" Es kamen nun im Frühjahr 1942 die ersten Transporte aus Oberschlesien, die alle zu vernichten waren. Sie gingen auch zuerst ganz ruhig in die Räume, in denen sie desinfiziert werden sollten Bis dann einige doch stutzig wurden und von Ersticken, von Vernichten sprachen. Es entstand dann sofort eine Art Panik. Doch schnell wurden die noch draussen stehenden in die Kammern hineingetrieben und die Türen zugeschraubt. Bei den nächsten Transporten wurde von vornherein nach den unruhigen Geistern gefahndet und diese nicht aus den Augen gelassen. Machte sich Unruhe bemerkbar, so wurden die Unruheverbrei-

"Brutality in Stone"

The 1960 film *Brutality in Stone [Brutalität in Stein]* by Alexander Kluge and Peter Schamoni indicated a renewed reflection on Nazi buildings. Using the workbook's precise instructions regarding picture, editing and sound, the architecture was to be deconstructed.

↑ Workbook (replica)
Schamoni Film & Medien München

Hermann Glaser on the opening of the exhibition
in the Zeppelin Grandstand 1984

"We hesitated about the grounds because we thought they should be allowed to fall into ruin."

↗ Pädagogisches Institut: Faszination und Gewalt. Ein Bericht, Nürnberg 1985
↓ Hermann Glaser 1965, Nürnberger Nachrichten/Gertrud Gerardi

Hermann Glaser
1928–2018

Influenced by childhood experiences in the Nazi era, Nuremberg's cultural officer Professor Hermann Glaser initiated the *Nuremberg Discussions [Nürnberger Gespräche]* in the 1960s. Many intellectuals, including Jewish emigrants like Fritz Stern and Jean Améry, pondered over historical and political issues.

Under Glaser's aegis, the *Fascination and Violence [Faszination und Gewalt]* exhibition opened in the Zeppelin Grandstand in 1984. Nationally acclaimed, despite criticism of the content, the exhibition was regarded as the first step towards engaging with the rally grounds. Until his death in 2018, Glaser remained a committed champion of *socioculture* and was author of many publications on German cultural history.

Discussion panel

In the *Nuremberg Discussions* Hermann Glaser addressed a question posed by the 1968 generation: How could the *Third Reich* happen? The packed Meistersingerhalle in the 1960s evidenced the great interest in the subject.

↑ Nuremberg Discussion, in the Meistersingerhalle 1965
Nürnberger Nachrichten/Gertrud Gerardi

First Exhibition "Fascination and Terror"

In 1985, Nuremberg's Pädagogische Institut put together the exhibition *Fascination and Terror [Faszination und Gewalt].* Its panels were of an intentionally provisional nature. The exhibition (in German), could only be viewed in the summer in the unheated Zeppelin Grandstand, but it attracted well over 50,000 visitors. It closed in 2001 with the opening of the Documentation Centre.

← *Faszination und Gewalt* poster 1992
Stadtarchiv Nürnberg A28-1992_0561_1

→ *Faszination und Gewalt* exhibition panel 1985
Dokumentationszentrum Reichsparteitagsgelände DZO-0145-01/
exhibit photography: Stefan Meyer

↓ *Faszination und Gewalt* exhibition room 1985
Stadtarchiv Nürnberg A40-L_4475_3

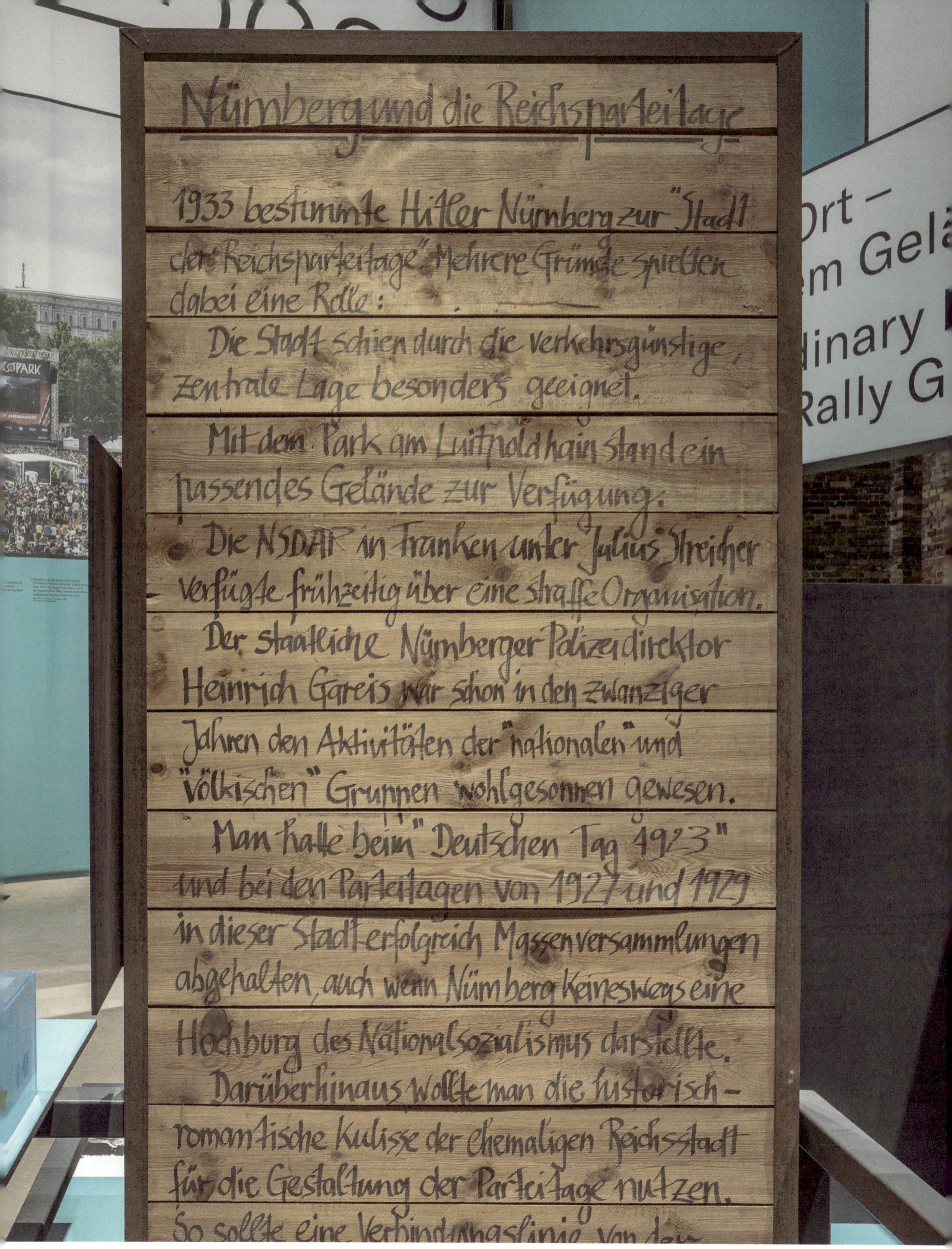
Nürnberg und die Reichsparteitage
1933 bestimmte Hitler Nürnberg zur "Stadt
der Reichsparteitage". Mehrere Gründe spielten
dabei eine Rolle:
Die Stadt schien durch die verkehrsgünstige,
zentrale Lage besonders geeignet.
Mit dem Park am Luitpoldhain stand ein
passendes Gelände zur Verfügung.
Die NSDAP in Franken unter Julius Streicher
verfügte frühzeitig über eine straffe Organisation.
Der staatliche Nürnberger Polizeidirektor
Heinrich Gareis war schon in den zwanziger
Jahren den Aktivitäten der "nationalen" und
"völkischen" Gruppen wohlgesonnen gewesen.
Man hatte beim "Deutschen Tag 1923"
und bei den Parteitagen von 1927 und 1929
in dieser Stadt erfolgreich Massenversammlungen
abgehalten, auch wenn Nürnberg keineswegs eine
Hochburg des Nationalsozialismus darstellte.
Darüberhinaus wollte man die historisch-
romantische Kulisse der ehemaligen Reichsstadt
für die Gestaltung der Parteitage nutzen.
So sollte eine

Documentation Center

In 2001, Nuremberg set a prominent example with the Documentation Center. Architect Günther Domenig sliced right through the listed building and topped it with the obliquely angled structure of the study forum, deliberately flouting the monumental severity of the Congress Hall.

↑ Entrance to the Documentation Center 2020
Dokumentationszentrum Reichsparteitagsgelände D-0310-01/
Nürnberg Luftbild Hajo Dietz

Günther Domenig, on his first encounter with the Congress Hall in 1998

"... power translated into architecture – it was all right angles and axes. I wanted to destroy that power."

↗ Günther Domenig in 2000, Dokumentationszentrum Reichsparteitagsgelände Ph-1138-13
↓ Press release Dokumentationszentrum Reichsparteitagsgelände 2001

Günther Domenig
1934–2012

Günther Domenig was one of Austria's most important contemporary architects. Radical, consistent and visionary, his work won many awards. He always regarded architecture as a gesamtkunstwerk and as a political statement.

In 1998, Domenig won the international architecture competition for the Documentation Center in Nuremberg. According to Günther Domenig his parents harboured Nazi sympathies. The Nuremberg project was therefore part of an engagement with his own biography.

Glass Corridor

A 130-metre long corridor of glass and steel cuts through the north wing of the Congress Hall as a walk-in exhibit. The spear-like corridor ends in an observation platform overlooking the interior courtyard.

← Glass corridor Documentation Center 2013
Dokumentationszentrum Reichsparteitagsgelände D-0311-01/
Helmut Meyer zur Capellen

Tourist Attraction

The grounds have always attracted visitors interested in the history of the buildings. However, in the decades immediately after the war, sources of information were scarce. Concerned about attracting right-wing elements, the city of Nuremberg was for a long time reluctant to officially cater for tourism on the grounds.

It was only in the 1980s that brochures, tours and the first exhibition provided a suitable service. To some extent criticism of commercial and superficial memorial tourism is justified. However, many guests display a serious interest in the subject. The Documentation Center alone attracts more than 300,000 visitors annually.

"On the Hitler Trail"

In the 1970s, the press ran articles about tourists *on the Hitler Trail*. For a long time, the city hoped that this type of interest in dark tourism would die a natural death. Today, visitors are offered many options of gaining a deeper knowledge of historical events, taking them beyond morbid fascination.

→ Excerpt from Heinz Günther: Was geschieht mit der Kongreßhalle? in: Abendblatt – 8-Uhr-Blatt 21.8.1971
Dokumentationszentrum Reichsparteitagsgelände D-0316-02

Die Touristen sind das größte Problem von Ernst Maier (53), der im Auftrag des städtischen Liegenschaftsamtes eine Art Hausmeister für das einstige Parteitagsgelände ist. (Maier: „Jahr für Jahr kommen Tausende Touristen zu mir, um sich den Rundbau und das ganze Gelände zeigen zu lassen. Engländer, Holländer und Franzosen, vor allem aber Amerikaner, die auf Hitlers Spuren wandeln wollen. Die sprechen mich überall an. Aber es fällt mir leicht, mit den Schultern zu zucken, denn ich verstehe tatsächlich keine Fremdsprache. Nur manchmal, wenn Generäle und Admiräle kommen, offiziell, dann springe ich als Fremdenführer ein.“

In seinem atombombensicheren Minibüro im Erdgeschoß des Superbaus hat Hausmeister Maier 24 Jahre lang hinter meterdicken Granitmauern über

Nürnberg (E
Zeugnis einer
Provinzstadt m
Stadtvätern, di
den Touristen,

das alles nachde
Ihm geht es imm
jedem Fremden,
bergern ganz zu
irrer Riese hat h
geklotzt, auf das n
vernünftigen R
kann. Ist das G
tonisch bewunde
historisch geseher
Soll das alles als
Zeugnis erhalten
genutzt oder wo S
los ist — dem la
fall preisgegeben

Das Sprengen a
anders als bei der
men — beim Run

Nuremberg Highlights

The tourist industry soon discovered the attraction of the grounds for tourists. In the 2000s the Palace of Justice, scene of the *Nuremberg Trials*, together with the Congress Hall, joined mediaeval sights on postcards.

↑ Postcard *Nürnberg* 2008
Dokumentationszentrum Reichsparteitagsgelände D-0316-01

DOKUMENTATIONSZENTRUM Reichsparteitagsgelände

Unsere Angebots-Pakete in Nürnberg

Nürnbergs verpflichtende Vergangenheit

Die Zeit von 1933 bis 1945 beschreibt das dunkelste Kapitel der Stadt Nürnberg. Das Dokumentationszentrum Reichsparteitagsgelände vermittelt die Geschichte der Reichsparteitage und analysiert die Zusammenhänge und Folgen der Gewaltherrschaft. Als größter Meilenstein in der Geschichte des Völkerrechts gelten hingegen die Nürnberger Prozesse. Am historischen Ort ist seit 2010 mit dem Memorium Nürnberger Prozesse eine Dokumentationsstätte wieder zugänglich, die über die Prozesse und die internationalen Nachwirkungen aufklärt.

3 für 2 SPECIAL

Leistungen:

- eine, zwei oder drei Übernachtungen mit Frühstücksbuffet
- Eintritt in das Dokumentationszentrum Reichsparteitagsgelände
- Eintritt in das „Memorium Nürnberger Prozesse“
- Kurzführer „Reichsparteitagsgelände Nürnberg“

ab 65,- Euro

Gültigkeit:
1. Januar bis 26. November und 23. bis 31. Dezember 2015, ausgenommen Messezeiten (siehe Kalender im Umschlag)

Reise zum Nürnberger Christkind

Erleben Sie die Weihnachtsstadt Nr. 1 mit dem berühmten Christkindlesmarkt und tauchen Sie ein in die unverwechselbare Atmosphäre der festlich geschmückten Altstadt.

Unser Tipp: Reisen Sie am Sonntag an und genießen Sie - wie es auch die Nürnberger machen - Ihren Bummel über den Christkindlesmarkt am Sonntagabend oder unter der Woche.

Leistungen:

- eine, zwei oder drei Übernachtungen mit Frühstücksbuffet
- Nürnberger Weihnachts-Pass mit Gutscheinen für:
  - einen Nürnberger Elisen-Lebkuchen
  - einen Glühwein mit Sammeltasse
  - ein Bratwurstbrötchen
  - Eintritt in die Krippenausstellung in St. Egidien
  - Bildpostkarte vom Nürnberger Christkind
  - 2 € Nachlass auf die Christkindlesmarkt-DVD
- ein Weihnachtssouvenir

ab 66,- Euro

Gültigkeit:
27. November bis 23. Dezember 2015

DTM-Highlight am Norisring

Das Highlight der DTM-Serie ist der spektakuläre Stadtkurs am Norisring. Für alle Motorsport-Begeisterten haben wir ein exklusives DTM-Event-Paket geschnürt, in dem alles beinhaltet ist, was Sie für ein spannendes Rennwochenende benötigen.

Leistungen:

- zwei Übernachtungen in einem Mittelklasse-Hotel mit Frühstücksbuffet
- ein Wochenend-Ticket für das DTM-Rennen auf dem Norisring (wahlweise Silber oder Gold)
- Ticket für den öffentlichen Nahverkehr
- ein Stadtrundgang oder ein schriftlicher Stadtführer
- die Original Nürnberger Rostbratwürstchen in einem Altstadtrestaurant

➙ tourismus.nuernberg.de/norisring

2 Übernachtungen ab 185,- Euro

Gültigkeit:
voraussichtlich 26. bis 28. Juni 2015

Nürnberg zum Verschenken

Sie nennen uns den Geldwert, den Sie verschenken wollen und bekommen von uns einen repräsentativen Gutschein.

GESCHENK-GUTSCHEIN

Pakete und Hotels in Fürth ab Seite 101 - Pakete und Hotel in Erlangen ab Seite 112 - Paket und Hotel in Schwabach Seite 117

07

Tourist Package

In the not so distant past, Nuremberg's binding legacy was available as a low-cost package alongside the Christmas Market and Norisring Car Race, as part of the city's official offers for tourists. New brochures address the historical site with greater sensitivity.

↑ *Reiseerlebnisse* catalogue 2015
Congress- und Tourismus-Zentrale Nürnberg

Binding Legacy?

Nuremberg confronts its past: In 1995, 60 years after the passing of the *Nuremberg Laws* and 50 years after the end of the war, the *International Nuremberg Human Rights Award* was bestowed for the first time. It was intended as a response to Nuremberg's Nazi legacy and the crimes committed at the time. Important permanent sources of information were created with the opening of the Documentation Centre in 2001 and Memorium Nuremberg Trials in 2010.

However, remembrance culture can encompass more: appropriate memorial sites for victims of National Socialism, an on-going discourse on approaches to the rally grounds and the responsibility of the individual within the urban community.

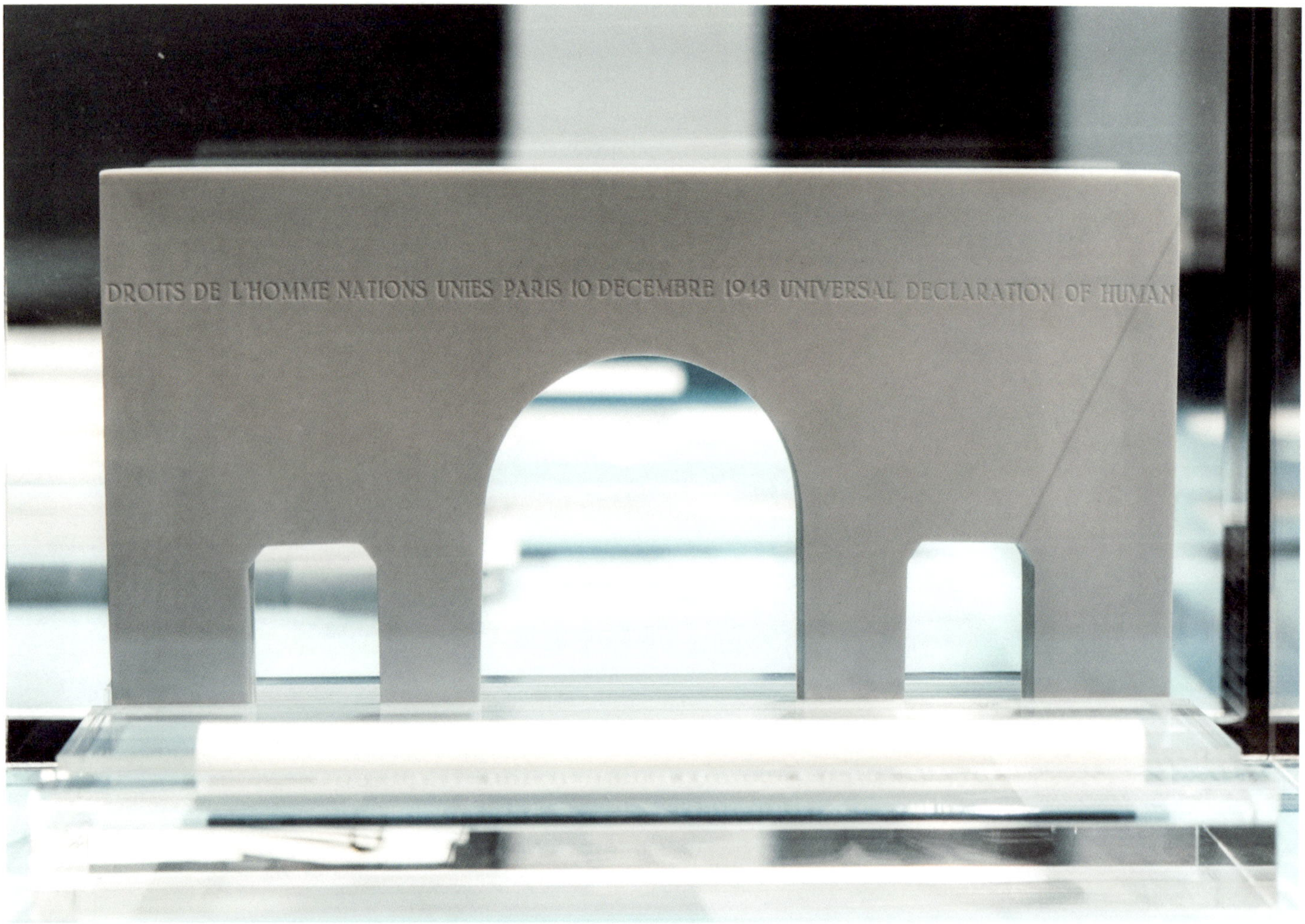

Nuremberg Human Rights Award

The biennial award is bestowed on defenders of human rights. The sculpture recalls the *Way of Human Rights [Straße der Menschenrechte]* by Israeli artist Dani Karavan and symbolises hope for a world that respects human rights.

↑ Award sculpture 1995
Stadt Nürnberg, Menschenrechtsbüro/exhibit photography: Christian Sperber

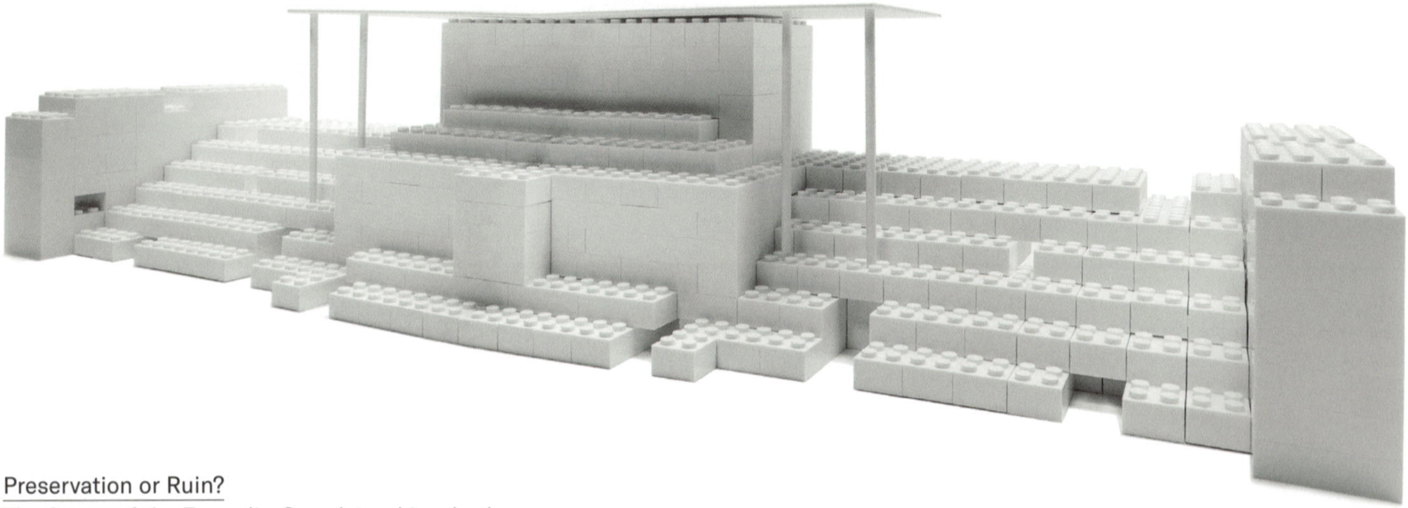

Preservation or Ruin?

The future of the Zeppelin Grandstand is a hotly discussed topic in the city. In 2014 Lego models visualised various ways of dealing with the building in the future.

↑ Lego grandstand 2014
BauLust e.V., Positionen 2014

March Field Station

In 2006, information boards were erected at the former March Field station. Despite committed civic initiatives, the disused station is still not a worthy place of remembrance of captivity, forced labour and deportation.

↑ March Field station 2020
Dokumentationszentrum Reichsparteitagsgelände D-0334

Abiding Images

Collective Visual Memory

Today, the pictures of Leni Riefenstahl and Heinrich Hoffmann are rooted in the collective visual memory. For decades they were used uncritically as illustrations in documentations, academic papers and textbooks on National Socialism, perpetuating the idea of "omnipotent" propaganda and "seduced" Germans. The staged propaganda images of the Nazi era have influenced the history preception of generations up to the present day.

The once innovative film aesthetics of *Triumph of the Will* are used in many modern feature films. Shots of massed parades reference the 1934 film in different contexts. Meanwhile, it is customary among historians and in documentaries to address the origins and intentions of the images with a critical eye.

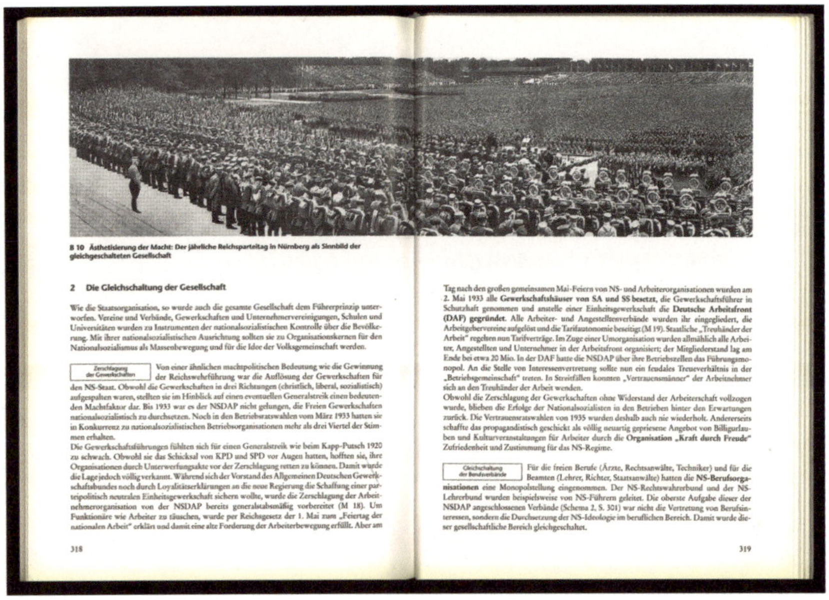

B 10 Ästhetisierung der Macht: Der jährliche Reichsparteitag in Nürnberg als Sinnbild der gleichgeschalteten Gesellschaft

2 Die Gleichschaltung der Gesellschaft

Wie die Staatsorganisation, so wurde auch die gesamte Gesellschaft dem Führerprinzip unterworfen. Vereine und Verbände, Gewerkschaften und Unternehmervereinigungen, Schulen und Universitäten wurden zu Instrumenten der nationalsozialistischen Kontrolle über die Bevölkerung. Mit ihrer nationalsozialistischen Ausrichtung sollten sie zu Organisationskernen für den Nationalsozialismus als Massenbewegung und für die Idee der Volksgemeinschaft werden.

Zerschlagung der Gewerkschaften

Von einer ähnlichen machtpolitischen Bedeutung wie die Gewinnung der Reichswehrführung war die Auflösung der Gewerkschaften für den NS-Staat. Obwohl die Gewerkschaften in drei Richtungen (christlich, liberal, sozialistisch) aufgespalten waren, stellten sie im Hinblick auf einen eventuellen Generalstreik einen bedeutenden Machtfaktor dar. Bis 1933 war es der NSDAP nicht gelungen, die Freien Gewerkschaften nationalsozialistisch zu durchsetzen. Noch in den Betriebsratswahlen vom März 1933 hatten sie in Konkurrenz zu nationalsozialistischen Betriebsorganisationen mehr als drei Viertel der Stimmen erhalten.
Die Gewerkschaftsführungen fühlten sich für einen Generalstreik wie beim Kapp-Putsch 1920 zu schwach. Obwohl sie das Schicksal von KPD und SPD vor Augen hatten, hofften sie, ihre Organisationen durch Unterwerfungsakte vor der Zerschlagung retten zu können. Damit wurde die Lage jedoch völlig verkannt. Während sich der Vorstand des Allgemeinen Deutschen Gewerkschaftsbundes noch durch Loyalitätserklärungen an die neue Regierung die Schaffung einer parteipolitisch neutralen Einheitsgewerkschaft sichern wollte, wurde die Zerschlagung der Arbeitnehmerorganisation von der NSDAP bereits generalstabsmäßig vorbereitet (M 18). Um Funktionäre wie Arbeiter zu täuschen, wurde per Reichsgesetz der 1. Mai zum „Feiertag der nationalen Arbeit" erklärt und damit eine alte Forderung der Arbeiterbewegung erfüllt. Aber am

318

Tag nach den großen gemeinsamen Mai-Feiern von NS- und Arbeiterorganisationen wurden am 2. Mai 1933 alle **Gewerkschaftshäuser von SA und SS besetzt**, die Gewerkschaftsführer in Schutzhaft genommen und anstelle einer Einheitsgewerkschaft die **Deutsche Arbeitsfront (DAF) gegründet**. Alle Arbeiter- und Angestelltenverbände wurden ihr eingegliedert, die Arbeitgebervereine aufgelöst und die Tarifautonomie beseitigt (M 19). Staatliche „Treuhänder der Arbeit" regelten nun Tarifverträge. Im Zuge einer Umorganisation wurden allmählich alle Arbeiter, Angestellten und Unternehmer in der Arbeitsfront organisiert; der Mitgliederstand lag am Ende bei etwa 20 Mio. In der DAF hatte die NSDAP über ihre Betriebszellen das Führungsmonopol. An die Stelle von Interessenvertretung sollte nun ein feudales Treueverhältnis in der „Betriebsgemeinschaft" treten. In Streitfällen konnten „Vertrauensmänner" der Arbeitnehmer sich an den Treuhänder der Arbeit wenden.
Obwohl die Zerschlagung der Gewerkschaften ohne Widerstand der Arbeiterschaft vollzogen wurde, blieben die Erfolge der Nationalsozialisten in den Betrieben hinter den Erwartungen zurück. Die Vertrauensratswahlen von 1935 wurden deshalb auch nie wiederholt. Andererseits schaffte das propagandistisch geschickt als völlig neuartig gepriesene Angebot von Billigurlauben und Kulturveranstaltungen für Arbeiter durch die **Organisation „Kraft durch Freude"** Zufriedenheit und Zustimmung für das NS-Regime.

Gleichschaltung der Berufsverbände

Für die freien Berufe (Ärzte, Rechtsanwälte, Techniker) und für die Beamten (Lehrer, Richter, Staatsanwälte) hatten die **NS-Berufsorganisationen** eine Monopolstellung eingenommen. Der NS-Rechtswahrerbund und der NS-Lehrerbund wurden beispielsweise von NS-Führern geleitet. Die oberste Aufgabe dieser der NSDAP angeschlossenen Verbände (Schema 2, S. 301) war nicht die Vertretung von Berufsinteressen, sondern die Durchsetzung der NS-Ideologie im beruflichen Bereich. Damit wurde dieser gesellschaftliche Bereich gleichgeschaltet.

319

Illustrations

In exhibitions and textbooks well into the 2000s, propaganda photos of the rallies were unrelated to the text and influenced the viewers' interpretation of the events.

← History textbooks 1998
Private property

→ *Fascination and Terror* exhibition sign, Documentation Center 2001–2021, with various school textbooks and *Riefenstahl-Reception* monitor
Dokumentationszentrum Reichsparteitagsgelände DZO-0150/
exhibit photography: Christian Sperber

Der „Führer“
707
Die Parteitagsregie war ganz auf
den „Führer“ und den „Führermythos“
zugeschnitten. Auch dies wurde
durch die Architektur unterstrichen.
Der König der Löwen
Zeichentrickfilm, USA 1994
Walt Disney Company

Art on the Grounds

In various ways, art can enable new approaches and expand perceptions of the rally grounds. For decades, artists have sought personal answers to questions of remembrance, guilt and appropriate ways of engaging with the architectural legacy of the Nazis.

Accompanying the exhibition in the Zeppelin Grandstand in 1985 and since, artistic presentations have taken place on the grounds. In 2004, a city council guideline paper expressly envisaged a role for art on the grounds. Nevertheless, since the 1990s little has taken place in this vein. Sustained interest in artistic engagement and specific inquiries in recent years confirm the need for a conceptual framework to promote art on the grounds in the future.

Theatre

In 2009 Staatstheater Nürnberg performed *The Investigation [Die Ermittlung]* by Peter Weiss in the Congress Hall. The impressive performance in the unusual atmospheric setting of the former Quelle warehouse changed perceptions of the play and the venue.

↑ Theatre performance *Die Ermittlung* in the Congress Hall 2009
Staatstheater Nürnberg/Marion Bührle

1980

Title — The Anachronistic Train or Freedom and Democracy
Artist — Aktion Brecht versus Strauß with Hanne Hiob
Venue — In front of the Zeppelin Grandstand

1980

Title — Overkill I and II
Artist — Hans Jürgen Breuste
Venue — Rear of Zeppelin Grandstand

1986

Title — The Commentary of the Living on the Dead Traces of the Past
Artist — Einstürzende Neubauten
Venue — Zeppelin Grandstand Hall

1988

Title — Lodz
Artist — Hans Jürgen Breuste
Venue — Zeppelin Grandstand Hall

Symbolic Place: Zeppelin Grandstand

The former rally grounds and Zeppelin Grandstand in particular are no ordinary places. They are not appropriate as innocent backdrops for Instagram posts or provocative stages on the web. The question arises: How much trivialisation do we allow?

This place is important for the survivors of the crimes of National Socialism and for their descendants. They can express satisfaction that wrongs have been redressed and call for an increased engagement with history. However, this place is also important to us as a democratic society. It constantly presents us with a challenge. We have to take a stand and seek our own way of dealing with the architectural legacy of National Socialism. Radical right-wing crimes and political movements since 1945 show that the story is not finished.

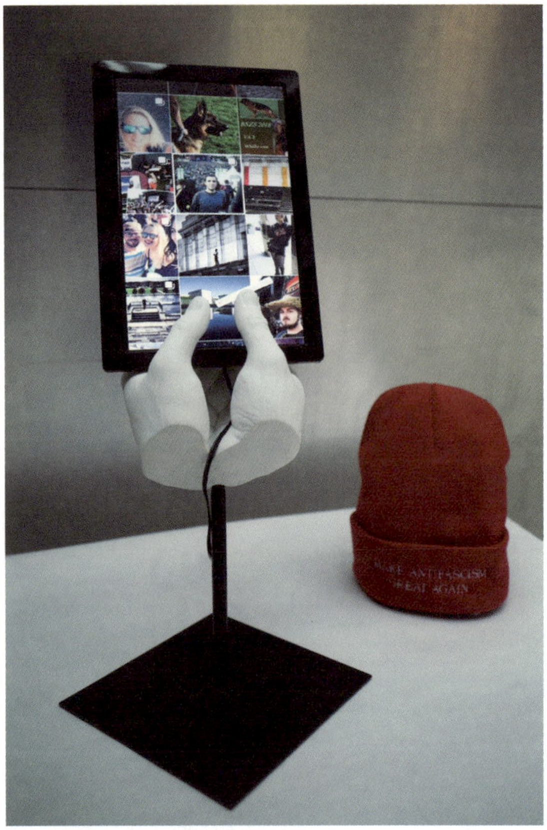

"rise and fall and fail and scroll"

Visual artist Sebastian Tröger trawled the Web for evidential material and his 2021 installation shows how diversely the rally grounds are perceived and staged by different groups.

↑ Sebastian Tröger: *rise and fall and fail and scroll* 2021
Dokumentationszentrum Reichsparteitagsgelände DZO-0151/
exhibit photography: Sebastian Tröger

NSU Murders

When, in July 2018 the sentences were pronounced on the members of the *National Socialist Underground [Nationalsozialistischen Untergrund]*, this exhortation was sprayed on the Zeppelin Grandstand. In Nuremberg, the NSU committed three murders in the immediate vicinity of the rally grounds – a coincidence?

→ Graffiti *No more NSU* on the Zeppelin Grandstand 2018
Dokumentationszentrum Reichsparteitagsgelände D-0313

NIE
WIEDER
NSU

"Pride and Satisfaction"
Leon Weintraub survived the Holocaust and has often taken part in contemporary witness interviews at the Documentation Center. The former podium is an important place for him.

↑ Leon Weintraub on the Zeppelin Grandstand 2012
Dokumentationszentrum Reichsparteitagsgelände D-0312

Leon Weintraub, Holocaust survivor,
on a visit to the Zeppelin Grandstand 2012

"As I stood up there, on this Zeppelin Grandstand [...], I was gripped by a feeling of unreality [...]. But mixed with a little pride and satisfaction that I was standing where Hitler had stood and received the homage of his followers during the parades."

in: Alexander Schmidt (Hg.): Das Gelände, Nürnberg 2015

Recommended reading

André François-Poncet: Botschafter in Berlin, Mainz 1948.

Angrick, Andrej/Klein, Peter: Die „Endlösung“ in Riga. Ausbeutung und Vernichtung 1941–1944, Darmstadt 2006.

Auerbach, Hellmuth: Regionale Wurzeln und Differenzen der NSDAP 1919–1923, in: Möller, Horst/Wirsching, Andreas/Ziegler, Walter (Hg.): Nationalsozialismus in der Region. Beiträge zur regionalen und lokalen Forschung und zum internationalen Vergleich, München 1996, S. 65–85.

Bauernfeind, Martina/Windsheimer, Bernd: Langwasser. Geschichte eines Stadtteils, Nürnberg 2007.

Beer, Helmut/Heyden, Thomas/Loch, Christian/Liedtke, Gerd-Dieter/Nerdinger, Winfried/Schmidt, Alexander: Bauen in Nürnberg 1933–1945. Architektur und Bauformen im Nationalsozialismus, Nürnberg 1995.

Bennewitz, Nadja/Franger, Gabriele (Hg.): Geschichte der Frauen in Mittelfranken. Alltag, Personen, Orte, Cadolzburg 2003.

Benz, Wolfgang/Diefenbacher Michael (Hg.): Die steinerne Rose. Erinnerungen einer polnischen Fremdarbeiterin in Deutschland 1942–1943, von Barbara Ostyn (Jablonska), Berlin 2003.

Benz, Wolfgang/Distel, Barbara (Hg.): Der Ort des Terrors. Geschichte der nationalsozialistischen Konzentrationslager, Bd. 9, München 2009.

Boeckl, Matthias (Hg.): Günther Domenig. Recent Work, Wien 2005.

Braun, Matthias Klaus: Hitlers liebster Bürgermeister: Willy Liebel (1897–1945) (Nürnberger Werkstücke zur Stadt- und Landesgeschichte 71), Nürnberg 2012.

Brechtken, Magnus: Speer – eine deutsche Karriere, Berlin 2017.

Breloer, Heinrich: Die Akte Speer. Spuren eines Kriegsverbrechers, Berlin 2005.

Brockhaus, Gudrun (Hg.): Attraktion der NS-Bewegung, Essen 2014.

Browning, Christopher: Die Entfesselung der Endlösung. Nationalsozialistische Judenpolitik 1939–1942, München 2003.

Christmeier Martina/Schmidt, Alexander (Hg.): Albert Speer in der Bundesrepublik. Vom Umgang mit deutscher Vergangenheit, Petersberg 2017.

Dietzfelbinger, Eckhart/Liedtke, Gerhard: Nürnberg – Ort der Massen. Das Reichsparteitagsgelände: Vorgeschichte und schwieriges Erbe, Berlin 2004.

Dokumentationszentrum NS-Zwangsarbeit der Stiftung Topographie des Terrors (Hg.): Zwischen allen Stühlen. Die Geschichte der Italienischen Militärinternierten 1943–1945, Berlin 2016.

Dokumentationszentrum NS-Zwangsarbeit der Stiftung Topographie des Terrors (Hg.): Alltag Zwangsarbeit 1938–1945, Berlin 2013.

Dokumentationszentrum Reichsparteitagsgelände/Geschichte Für Alle e.V./Bunter Tisch Gartenstadt und Siedlungen Süd (Hg.): VON AUSCHWITZ NACH NÜRNBERG. Das KZ-Außenlager der Siemens-Schuckertwerke, Nürnberg 2020.

Doosry, Yasmin: „Wohlauf, laßt uns eine Stadt und einen Turm bauen …“. Studien zum Reichsparteitagsgelände in Nürnberg, Tübingen 2002.

Echternkamp, Jörg (Hg.): Das Deutsche Reich und der Zweite Weltkrieg, Bd. 9/2, Staat und Gesellschaft im Kriege: Die deutsche Kriegsgesellschaft 1939 bis 1945 – Ausbeutung, Deutungen, Ausgrenzung, München 2005.

Ehresmann, Andreas (Hg.): Das Stalag X B Sandbostel. Geschichte und Nachgeschichte eines Kriegsgefangenenlagers, München/Hamburg 2015.

Endres, Rudolf/Fleischmann, Martina: Nürnbergs Weg in die Moderne: Wirtschaft, Politik und Gesellschaft im 19. und 20. Jahrhundert, Nürnberg 1996.

Essner, Cornelia: Die „Nürnberger Gesetze“ oder die Verwaltung des Rassenwahns 1933–1945, Paderborn 2002.

Fleischmann, Peter (Hg.): Hitler als Häftling in Landsberg am Lech 1923/24. Der Gefangenen-Personalakt Hitler nebst weiteren Quellen aus der Schutzhaft-, Untersuchungshaft- und Festungshaftanstalt, Neustadt/Aisch 2015.

Frommer, Hartmut/Westner, Kathrin: „Ein Justizcollegium weit schlimmer wie eine Diebsbande“. Die Vernichtung von Leo Katzenberger durch das Sondergericht Nürnberg, in: MVGN 85 (1998), S. 315–326.

Gerhard Jochem/Ulrike Kettner (Bearb.): Gedenkbuch für die Nürnberger Opfer der Shoa, Nürnberg 1998.

Gerstenberg, Günther: Sozialistische Arbeiterjugend (SAJ), 1922–1933, publiziert am 13.07.2006; in: Historisches Lexikon Bayerns, URL: https://www.historisches-lexikon-bayerns.de/Lexikon/Sozialistische_Arbeiterjugend_(SAJ),_1922-1933 (25.01.2021).

Gerstenberg, Günther: Zweites Arbeiter-Turn- und Sportfest, Nürnberg, 18.–21. Juli 1929, publiziert am 13.07.2006; in: Historisches Lexikon Bayerns, URL: https://www.historisches-lexikon-bayerns.de/Lexikon/Zweites_Arbeiter-Turn-_und_Sportfest,_Nürnberg,_18.-21._Juli_1929 (25.01.2021).

Gregor, Neil: Haunted City. Nuremberg and the Nazi Past, New Haven/London/Yale 2008.

Gruber, Lilli: Das Erbe. Die Geschichte meiner Südtiroler Familie, München 2013.

Hambrecht, Rainer: Die braune Bastion: Der Aufstieg der NSDAP in Mittel- und Oberfranken (1922–1933), Petersberg 2017.

Hambrecht, Rainer: Die Brücke Franken. Franken – eine entscheidende Station auf Hitlers Weg von München nach Berlin, in: Hambrecht, Rainer/Mück, Wolfgang/Kett, Siegfried, Glaser/Hermann (Hg.): Das braune Franken. Hitlers Weg von München nach Berlin. Reihe Buchfranken 8 (2017), S. 9–38.

Hammermann, Gabriele/Riedle, Andrea (Hg.): Der Massenmord an den sowjetischen Kriegsgefangenen auf dem SS-Schießplatz Hebertshausen 1941–1942, Göttingen 2020.

Hammermann, Gabriele: Zwangsarbeit für den „Verbündeten". Die Arbeits- und Lebensbedingungen der italienischen Militärinternierten in Deutschland 1933–1945, Tübingen 2002.

Hanschel, Hermann: Oberbürgermeister Hermann Luppe: Nürnberger Kommunalpolitik in der Weimarer Republik (Nürnberger Forschungen 21), Nürnberg 1977.

Hänschen, Steffen: Das Transitghetto Izbica im System des Holocaust, Berlin 2018.

Herz, Rudolf: Hoffmann und Hitler. Fotografie als Medium des Führer-Mythos, München 1994.

Heyden, Thomas: „Mit Doppel-F": Ludwig und Franz Ruff, in: Akademie der Bildenden Künste in Nürnberg (Hg..): Geartete Kunst – Die Nürnberger Akademie im Nationalsozialismus, Nürnberg 2012, S. 184–200.

https://de.wikipedia.org/wiki/Der_König_der_Löwen_(1994) (25.01.2021)

https://www.nuernberg.de/internet/menschenrechte/ (20.01.2021)

https://www.statistik-des-holocaust.de/

Hübschmann, Ekkehard: Die Deportation von Juden aus Franken nach Riga, in: Frankenland. Zeitschrift für fränkische Landeskunde und Kulturpflege 56 (2004) 5, S. 344-369.

Janetzko, Maren: *Arisierungen* in Nürnberg – ein Überblick, in: Henkel, Matthias/Dietzfelbinger, Eckart (Hg..) Entrechtet. Entwürdigt. Beraubt. Die *Arisierung* in Nürnberg und Fürth. Ausstellungskatalog Dokumentationszentrum Reichsparteitagsgelände Nürnberg. Petersberg 2012, S. 41–55.

Jochem, Gerhard: Feind bleibt Feind! Kriegsgefangene in Nürnberg 1939–1945, in: Mitteilungen des Vereins für Geschichte der Stadt Nürnberg 93 (2006), S. 227–298.

Karl, Michaela: „Ich blätterte gerade in der Vogue, da sprach mich der Führer an." Unity Mitford. Eine Biographie, München 2018.

Katheder, Doris/Weiß, Matthias (Hg.): Jenseits der Faszination? Die Ausstellung zum Nationalsozialismus in der Nürnberger Zeppelintribüne 1984–2001. Mit Fotos von Regina Maria Suchy, Würzburg 2013.

Keller, Rolf: Sowjetische Kriegsgefangene im Deutschen Reich 1941/42. Behandlung und Arbeitseinsatz zwischen Vernichtungspolitik und kriegswirtschaftlichen Zwängen, Göttingen 2011.

Kießling, Friedrich/Schöllgen, Gregor (Hg.): Bilder für die Welt. Die Reichsparteitage der NSDAP im Spiegel der ausländischen Presse, Köln/Weimar/Wien 2006.

Knigge, Volkhard/Lüttgenau, Rikola-Gunnar/Wagner, Jens-Christian (Hg.): Zwangsarbeit. Die Deutschen, die Zwangsarbeiter und der Krieg. Begleitband zur internationalen Wanderausstellung der Stiftung Gedenkstätten Buchenwald und Mittelbau-Dora, Weimar 2010.

Kramer, Helmut/Uhl, Karsten/Wagner, Jens-Christian (Hg.): Zwangsarbeit im Nationalsozialismus und die Rolle der Justiz. Täterschaft, Nachkriegsprozesse und die Auseinandersetzung um Entschädigungsleistungen, Nordhausen 2007.

Kuchler, Christian (Hg.): NS-Propaganda im 21. Jahrhundert. Zwischen Verbot und öffentlicher Auseinandersetzung, Köln 2014.

Kuller, Christiane/Drecoll, Axel: Inszenierter Volkszorn, ausgebliebene Empörung und der Sturz Julius Streichers. Reaktionen auf die wirtschaftliche Ausplünderung der Juden, in: Sabrow, Martin (Hg.) Skandal und Diktatur. Formen öffentlicher Empörung im NS-Staat und in der DDR, Göttingen 2004, S. 77–101.

Kuller, Christiane: Der Führer in fremden Welten. Das Star-Wars Imperium als historisches Lehrstück, in: Zeithistorische Forschungen/Studies in Contemporary History, Online-Ausgabe, 3 (2006) 1, URL: https://zeithistorische-forschungen.de/1-2006/4573 (25.01.2021).

Kunsthalle Nürnberg (Hg.): Das Gelände, Nürnberg 2008.

KZ-Gedenkstätte Flossenbürg (Hg.): Konzentrationslager Flossenbürg 1938–1945, Göttingen 2008.

Leßau, Hanne (Hg.): Das Reichsparteitagsgelände im Krieg. Gefangenschaft, Zwangsarbeit und Massenmord, Petersberg 2021.

Lilla, Joachim: Staatsminister, leitende Verwaltungsträger und (NS-)Funktionsträger in Bayern 1918 bis 1945, URL: https://verwaltungs-handbuch.bayerische-landesbibliothek-online.de

Luppe, Hermann: Mein Leben (Quellen zur Geschichte und Kultur der Stadt Nürnberg 10), Nürnberg 1977.

Mai, Uwe: Kriegsgefangen in Brandenburg. Stalag III A in Luckenwalde 1939–1945, Berlin 1999.

May, Herbert (Hg.): Zwangsarbeit im ländlichen Franken 1939–1945, Bad Windsheim 2008.

Metzger, Pascal: Dutzendteich: Nürnbergs Freizeitareal, Nürnberg 2018.

Müller, Arnd: Geschichte der Juden in Nürnberg 1146–1945 (Beiträge zur Geschichte und Kultur der Stadt Nürnberg 12), Nürnberg 1968.

Munzinger Online/Personen – Internationales Biographisches Archiv, URL: http://www.munzinger.de

Museen der Stadt Nürnberg (Hg.): Faszination und Gewalt. Dokumentationszentrum Reichsparteitagsgelände Nürnberg, Nürnberg 2006.

Ogan, Bernd/Weiß, Wolfgang W. (Hg.): Faszination und Gewalt. Zur politischen Ästhetik des Nationalsozialismus, Nürnberg 1992.

Otto, Reinhard/Keller, Ralf/Nagel, Jens: Sowjetische Kriegsgefangene in deutschem Gewahrsam 1941–1945. Zahlen und Dimensionen, in: Vierteljahreshefte für Zeitgeschichte 56 (2008) 4, S. 557–602.

Otto, Reinhard: Wehrmacht, Gestapo und sowjetische Kriegsgefangene im deutschen Reichsgebiet 1941/42, München 1998.

Paul, Gerhard/Mallmann, Klaus-Michael (Hg.): Die Gestapo im Zweiten Weltkrieg. „Heimatfront" und besetztes Europa, Darmstadt 2000.

Paul, Gerhard: Aufstand der Bilder. Die NS-Propaganda vor 1933, Bonn 1990.

Peters, Sebastian: Heinrich Hoffmann. Verlag nationalsozialistischer Bilder, publiziert am 27.11.2019; in: Historisches Lexikon Bayerns, URL: http://www.historisches-lexikon-bayerns.de/Lexikon/Heinrich_Hoffmann._Verlag_nationalsozialistischer_Bilder (18.02.2021)

Radlmaier, Dominik: Die lokale Machtübernahme in Nürnberg, in: Sauer, Christine (Hg.): „Für den deutschen – wider den undeutschen Geist". Von verbotener und regimekonformer Literatur im „Dritten Reich" (BCN Materialien – Ausstellungskatalog der Stadtbibliothek 106), Nürnberg 2013, S. 10–15.

Radlmaier, Dominik: Die Süßheims in Nürnberg. Geschichte der Familie und ihrer Sammlungen von den Gründerjahren bis in die NS-Zeit, in: Diefenbacher, Michael (Hg.): Die Süßheims. Unternehmer, Politiker, Wissenschaftler, Sammler (Quellen und Forschungen zur Geschichte und Kultur der Stadt Nürnberg 39), Nürnberg 2018, S. 55–197.

Radlmaier, Steffen/Zelnhefer, Siegfried: Tatort Nürnberg. Auf den Spuren des Nationalsozialismus, Cadolzburg 2002.

Rheinisches JournalistInnenbüro, Recherche International e.V. (Hg.): Unsere Opfer zählen nicht. Die Dritte Welt im Zweiten Weltkrieg, Berlin/Hamburg 2005.

Rohkrämer, Thomas: Die fatale Attraktion des Nationalsozialismus. Über die Popularität eines Unrechtsregimes, Paderborn 2013.

Sanden, Erika: Das Kriegsgefangenenlager Nürnberg-Langwasser. 1939–1945, Nürnberg 1993.

Sarkowicz, Hans: „Nur nicht langweilig werden ..." Das Radio im Dienst der nationalsozialistischen Propaganda, in: Heidenreich, Bernd/Neitzel, Sönke: Medien im Nationalsozialismus, Paderborn 2010, S. 205–234.

Schäfer, Anette: Zwangsarbeit in den Kommunen. „Ausländereinsatz" in Württemberg 1939–1945, in: Vierteljahreshefte für Zeitgeschichte 49 (2001) 1, S. 53–75.

Schmidt, Alexander (Hg.): Das Gelände. Dokumentation. Perspektiven. Diskussion. 1945–2015, Petersberg 2015.

Schmidt, Alexander: Das Reichsparteitagsgelände in Nürnberg, Nürnberg 2017.

Schmidt, Alexander: Kultur in Nürnberg 1918–1933: Die Weimarer Moderne in der Provinz, Nürnberg 2005.

Schmidt, Alexander: Weder braun noch schwarz. Tourismus auf dem ehemaligen Reichsparteitagsgelände, in: Quak, Hans-Dieter/Steinecke, Albrecht (Hg.): Dark Tourism. Faszination des Schreckens, Paderborn 2012, S. 171–191.

Schödel, Jutta: Die Russenwiese. Unveröff. Manuskript, Nürnberg 2015.

Schott, Herbert: Die ersten drei Deportationen mainfränkischer Juden 1941/42, in: Generaldirektion der Staatlichen Archive Bayerns (Hg.): Wege in die Vernichtung. Die Deportation der Juden aus Mainfranken 1941–1943, München 2003, S. 73–166.

Schott, Herbert: Filmaufnahmen der Judendeportationen aus Nürnberg 1941/42, in: Mitteilungen des Vereins für Geschichte der Stadt Nürnberg 98 (2011), S. 311–366.

Schott, Herbert: Julius Streicher und seine Bezeichnung als „Frankenführer", in: Jahrbuch für Fränkische Landesgeschichte 76 (2016), S. [277]–320.

Schul- und Kulturreferat der Stadt Nürnberg/Centrum Industriekultur (Hg.): Arbeitererinnerungen, Nürnberg 1984.

Schulz, Sonja M.: Der Nationalsozialismus im Film. Von Triumph des Willens bis Inglourious Bastards, Berlin 2012.

Seiderer, Georg: Nürnberg – die „Stadt der Reichsparteitage". Selbstinszenierung einer Großstadt im „Dritten Reich" (1933–1939), in: Mayrhofer, Fritz/Oppl, Ferdinand (Hg.): Stadt und Nationalsozialismus (Beiträge zur Geschichte der Städte Mitteleuropas XXI), Linz 2008, S. 311–340.

Shirer, William: Berliner Tagebuch, Leipzig 1994.

Shirer, William: The Rise And The Fall of the Third Reich, London 1998.

Sonnenberger, Franz: Faszination und Gewalt. Leitlinien für die Konzeption der neuen Dauerausstellung des Dokumentationszentrums Reichsparteitagsgelände, in: Museen der Stadt Nürnberg (Hg.): Die Zukunft der Vergangenheit. Wie soll Geschichte des Nationalsozialismus in Museen und Gedenkstätten im 21. Jahrhundert vermittelt werden?, Nürnberg 2000, S. 87–100.

Sösemann, Bernd: Das Medium „Fest" und seine kommunikationshistorische Bedeutung, o.J., URL: http://web.fu-berlin.de/akip/#aufsaetze (08.03.2021)

Stadt Nürnberg (Hg.): Rund um den Dutzendteich. Eine Nürnberger Stadtlandschaft im Wandel der Zeit, Nürnberg o.J. (2001).

Stadtarchiv Nürnberg (Bearb.): Schicksal jüdischer Mitbürger in Nürnberg 1933–1945, Nürnberg 1985.

Steuwer, Janosch: Das „Volk" vorzeigen: Die Reichsparteitage und die populistische Legitimation des Nationalsozialismus, in: Beigel, Thorsten/Eckert, Georg (Hg.): Populismus. Varianten von Volksherrschaft in Geschichte und Gegenwart, Münster 2017, S. 192–206.

Steuwer, Janosch: Was meint und nützt das Sprechen von der „Volksgemeinschaft"? Neuere Literatur zur Gesellschaftsgeschichte des Nationalsozialismus, in: Archiv für Sozialgeschichte 53 (2013), S. 487–534.

Studt, André/Schweneker, Claudia (Hg.): SchattenOrt: Theater auf dem Nürnberger Reichsparteitagsgelände. Ein Monument des NS-Größenwahns als Lernort und Bildungsmedium, Bielefeld 2013.

Süß, Dietmar: „Ein Volk, ein Reich, ein Führer". Die deutsche Gesellschaft im Dritten Reich, München 2017.

Täubrich, Hans-Christian (Hg.): Die Kongresshalle Nürnberg. Architektur und Geschichte, Petersberg 2014.

Täubrich, Hans-Christian (Hg.): Memorium Nürnberger Prozesse. Die Ausstellung, Nürnberg 2011.

Thamer, Hans-Ulrich: Politische Rituale und politische Kultur im Europa des 20. Jahrhunderts, in: Urban, Claus/ Engelhardt, Joachim (Hg.): Wirklichkeit im Zeitalter ihres Verschwindens, Münster 2000, S. 148–172.

Tobias, Jim G.: „... und wir waren Deutsche!" Jüdische Emigranten erinnern sich, Nürnberg 2009.

Urban, Markus: Die inszenierte Utopie. Zur Konstruktion von Gemeinschaft auf den Reichsparteitagen der NSDAP, in: Schmiechen-Ackermann, Detlef (Hg.): „Volksgemeinschaft": Mythos, wirkungsmächtige soziale Verheißung oder soziale Realität im „Dritten Reich"? Zwischenbilanz einer kontroversen Debatte, Paderborn u.a. 2012, S. 135–158.

Urban, Markus: Die Konsensfabrik. Funktion und Wahrnehmung der NS-Reichsparteitage 1933–1941, Göttingen 2007.

Wager, Melanie: „Nirgendwo ist unsere [...] Verfemung schlimmer und untragbarer als in Franken". Das Hetzblatt „Der Stürmer", in: Bildungsbüro der Stadt Nürnberg (Hg.) Menschenrechtslesebuch, Nürnberg 2014, S. 142–150.

Wager, Melanie: *Der Stürmer und seine Leser* – ein analoges (a-)soziales Netzwerk. Dissertation Friedrich-Alexander-Universität Erlangen-Nürnberg 2020, in Druck.

Wildt, Michael: Volksgemeinschaft als Selbstermächtigung. Gewalt gegen Juden in der deutschen Provinz 1919 bis 1939, Hamburg 2007.

Winkler, Heinrich August: Die deutsche Gesellschaft der Weimarer Republik und der Antisemitismus – Juden als „Blitzableiter", in: Benz, Wolfgang/Bergmann, Werner: Vorurteil und Völkermord. Entwicklungslinien des Antisemitismus, Freiburg/Breisgau 1997, S. 341–362.

Wodin, Natascha: Die gläserne Stadt, Cadolzburg 2017.

Zelnhefer, Siegfried: Deutscher Tag, Nürnberg, 1./2. September 1923, publiziert am 28.08.2006; in: Historisches Lexikon Bayerns, URL: https://www.historisches-lexikon-bayerns.de/Lexikon/Deutscher_Tag,_Nürnberg,_1./2._September_1923 (25.01.2021).

Zelnhefer, Siegfried: Die Reichsparteitage der NSDAP, Nürnberg 2002.

Zelnhefer, Siegfried: Willy Liebel, Oberbürgermeister der „Stadt der Reichsparteitage Nürnberg", in: Jahrbuch für Fränkische Landesgeschichte 60 (2000), S. 660–680.

Zinke, Peter: „An allem ist Alljuda schuld". Antisemitismus während der Weimarer Republik in Franken, Nürnberg 2009.

Imprint Exhibition

Nuremberg – Site of the Nazi Party Rallies
Staging, Experience and Violence

Interim Exhibition at the Documentation Center Nazi Party Rally Grounds
From 2021 to 2023
Large Exhibition Hall

Director, Dokumentationszentrum Reichsparteitagsgelände
Florian Dierl M.A.

Project Management
Dr Martina Christmeier, Dr Melanie Wager (Dokumentationszentrum Reichsparteitagsgelände, Nürnberg)

Curators
Dr Martina Christmeier, Nina Lutz M.A., Dr Melanie Wager (Dokumentationszentrum Reichsparteitagsgelände, Nürnberg)

Research Assistants
Dr Astrid Betz, Dr Alexander Schmidt (Dokumentationszentrum Reichsparteitagsgelände, Nürnberg)
Sebastian Peters M.A. (Institut für Zeitgeschichte, München-Berlin)

Project Assistant
Silvia Karg (Dokumentationszentrum Reichsparteitagsgelände, Nürnberg)

Design
Architecture: Rainer Lendler (Lendler Ausstellungsarchitektur, Berlin)
Graphic Design: (exhibition, catalogue, exterior): Jenny Hasselbach (Rimini Berlin)
Media Design: ("Changing Topography", projections, media stations): Jens Wunderling, Patrick Kochlik, Jan Scheffel (SYNTOP, Berlin)

Conservation Support
Paper: Annette Schubert (Handbuch – Atelier für Papiergestaltung, Nürnberg)
Textiles: Maria Ellinger-Gebhardt (Textilrestauratorin, Nürnberg)
Models: Markus Honka (NEOOS GmbH Interior Design + Modellbau, Nürnberg)

Creative Consulting/Audio Editing
Sebastian Tröger (Dokumentationszentrum Reichsparteitagsgelände, Nürnberg)

Drawings
Hamed Eshrat (Berlin)

Translation
Fiona Haberland M.A., Dr John Jenkins (Nürnberg)

Production and Set-up
Messebau Wörnlein (Nürnberg)
Lenticular Printing: Vogt Spezialdruck GmbH (Hessisch Lichtenau)

Exhibit Montage
Anette Schubert (Handbuch – Atelier für Papiergestaltung, Nürnberg)

Media and Electrical Installation/ Lighting, Logistics
Panagiotis Georgakopoulos, Tobias Richter, Armin Seubold (Dokumentationszentrum Reichsparteitagsgelände, Nürnberg)

Carpentry (step seats)
Herbert Einrichtungsbau (Nürnberg)

Press and Public Relations
Dr Martina Christmeier (Dokumentationszentrum Reichsparteitagsgelände, Nürnberg)
Tanja Heider M.A., Birgit Hohenstein M.A. (Museen der Stadt Nürnberg)

Educational Programme/ Supporting Events
Dr Astrid Betz (Dokumentationszentrum Reichsparteitagsgelände, Nürnberg)

Our special thanks go to the Nuremberg City Archives and the other archives, agencies, television stations, institutes, offices and departments of the City of Nuremberg, external colleagues, in particular Dr Hanne Leßau, as well as individuals, families and photographers, for their kind support in the mounting of this exhibition. Despite careful research, it was not possible to establish the owners of picture rights in all instances. In case of knowledge of the owners, the project managers request that they be contacted.

Imprint Catalogue

1st edition 2021

Publisher
Michael Imhof Verlag Gmbh & Co KG
Stettiner Straße 25, 36100 Petersberg
www.imhof-verlag.de

Published by
Dr Martina Christmeier, Dr Melanie Wager (Dokumentationszentrum Reichsparteitagsgelände, Nürnberg)

Concept and Editorial Work
Dr Martina Christmeier, Nina Lutz M.A., Dr Melanie Wager (Dokumentationszentrum Reichsparteitagsgelände, Nürnberg)

Project Assistant
Silvia Karg (Dokumentationszentrum Reichsparteitagsgelände, Nürnberg)

Translation
Fiona Haberland M.A., Dr John Jenkins (Nuremberg)

Graphic Design
Jenny Hasselbach (Rimini Berlin)

Printing
Schleunungdruck GmbH (Marktheidenfeld)

ISBN
978-3-7319-1146-3

Our thanks go to the Stiftung zur Unterstützung des Dokumentationszentrums Reichsparteitagsgelände for its generous support in the production of this catalogue.